Author: Stephanie Langston

M.Ed. Foreign Language Education
B.A. Spanish, A.B.J. Telecommunication Arts

Former Pharmacy Technician & Interpreter for Wal-Mart and Revco
Founder & President of Hands on Spanish, a language service company
Monroe, Georgia
Instructor of Spanish, Georgia Perimeter College
Covington, Georgia
Former Instructor of Spanish, The Georgia Institute of Technology
Atlanta, Georgia
Former Instructor of Spanish, Oxford College of Emory University
Oxford, Georgia

www.handsonspanish.com   770-856-0980

Note: This is a reference manual based on the Pharmacy Spanish Online Course. **Reading this reference manual and/or listening to the audio mp3 files will not provide CE credit.** You may obtain CE credit by taking the course online. The online course offers 12 hours of continuing education credit (1.2 CEU).

ACPE information for online program:
Pharmacists UAN: 0014-9999-11-074-H04-P   **Technicians** UAN: 0014-9999-11-074-H04-T
**Note: UAN numbers will be updated periodically as the course is renewed with the ACPE.

ACPE - Accreditation Statement

The University of Georgia College of Pharmacy is accredited by the Accreditation Council for Pharmacy Education as a provider of continuing pharmacy education.

Author: Stephanie Langston

I want to thank you for purchasing this manual! I hope that you find the program enjoyable and beneficial. I truly want you to have the best chance of succeeding with this program. On page eight of the manual you will find some tips for retention. One of the best things that you can do in order to learn a foreign language is to hear it spoken and to practice speaking it. This is why we have included the <u>complete digital audio course</u>. We hope that you will take advantage of it. We are also providing a coupon code for you to take the program online for 12 hours of ACPE credit at a discount (and/or to purchase the audio CDs at a discount).

Obtain Your Free Resources and Discounts! Visit:
www.handsonspanish.com/rx

FREE Resources:

1. Complete Digital Audio Course
Download the audio files to accompany the entire program.

2. Email Access to Author/Instructor
stephanie@handsonspanish.com

COUPON CODE for DISCOUNTED Resources:
Enter the code **RX217273** for a discount on the following:

12-hour ACPE Online Pharmacy Spanish Program

Audio CDs for the Entire Program

Forward

The course, *Pharmacy Spanish*, provides pharmacists and pharmacy technicians with knowledge and skills needed to provide a high level of care for Spanish-speaking patients and their families. In the day-to-day management of patients in any healthcare setting the clinician needs a quick reference for communicating with Spanish-speaking patients. The modular format delivers the content as manageable pieces of information and includes active learning exercises (¡Practiquemos! / Let's Practice!) that allow learners to demonstrate their understanding of the topic. This guide serves as a companion for the online course and is an excellent resource for visual learners. The online course includes assessments that provide feedback to the learner prior to moving onto the next lesson.

In this era of healthcare reform it is crucial for pharmacists (and pharmacy technicians) to cement their current role as well as expand into new roles. Patient counseling, medication therapy management, disease state management, and patient education are necessary functions of healthcare reform and the accessibility of pharmacists makes them highly suited to offer these services. In addition, immigration issues have impacted services delivered to some of our most vulnerable populations. Once again the accessibility of pharmacists creates the opportunity to provide care to all patients and this guide and companion course prepares pharmacists to deliver the care that is needed.

Stephanie Langston's teaching style is dynamic and versatile. She truly meets the needs of her learners through innovative teaching and learning techniques. Her background, education, and experience, as well as her professionalism have allowed her to provide a program that adds great value to our course offerings. I have found *Pharmacy Spanish* to be the right fit for our needs, including instruction for our students involved in the farm worker outreach program each summer.

Over a thousand registered pharmacists, pharmacy technicians, and pharmacy students have taken this course either in the online or face-to-face setting and have gained an understanding of how to provide care for Spanish-speaking patients and their families."

Trina von Waldner, Pharm.D.
Director, Continuing Education and Outreach
The University of Georgia College of Pharmacy

Testimonials

"The Hands on Spanish course was much more useful to my profession than other avenues that I have tried in the past. Stephanie Langston incorporates culture and professionalism in her lectures and proceeds forward to each level of the course with just enough speed. I was able to start speaking within about a week and I now feel very confident in my daily consultations. The program is truly catered to focus on all areas of the pharmacy, including insurance, patient complaints, regular counseling points such as how to take medications appropriately and side effect management. I strongly recommend this course to all pharmacy staff, as it truly makes a difference in the relationships that we have with our Spanish-speaking population."

             Suapna S. Pahalan, Pharm. D, CPh.
             Pharmacy Manager, Oncology Specialy Pharmacy, LLC
             Miami, Florida

"As a pharmacist working in a rural North Carolina hospital, I needed a way to better communicate with my Spanish speaking patients without the availability of an interpreter. Hands on Spanish, with its interactive online courses, quizzes, and web videos, was a fast and easy way to learn the basics about medically related topics not covered in introductory Spanish classes. Having taken Spanish both in high school and in college, I still found the background information on grammar very informative and a great refresher. After some practice, I have been able to give clear discharge instructions, perform accurate medication reconciliation, educate our asthmatics, and even assist the other staff in completing a patient history report. As recognition of this and other achievements, I received an increased annual bonus and now the physicians ask for me by name when they need help discussing medication issues!"

             Kristen Smith, R.Ph.

"I wanted to take the opportunity to tell you what an awesome time I am having in learning Pharmacy Spanish! My background is 4 years of high school Spanish and 1 year of undergraduate Spanish many, many years ago. Yet, I still learned new things with Hands on Spanish! Thank you! You have a wonderful program -- keep up the great work!

             Carolyn E. Matteo, R.Ph., Ph.D.
             Curadora Herida Healthcare Services

"I just completed the Pharmacy Spanish CE and wanted to let you know that I thought it was "muy bueno!" I have spoken Spanish for many years with education in middle/high school and college but my opportunities to use it have not been enough. This was a great refresher and I learned new information as well. Thank you for putting together such a great program!"

             Miranda Crown, R.Ph., Pharm.D., Rite Aid

"The approach helped me dig into the subject more deeply. I learned a great deal. There was a simplified language approach. Her manner of presentation makes the user feel comfortable. It has helped me to unravel some of the complexities of the language to make it practical. She made me feel more comfortable with pronunciation.
The program taught pertinent communication with customers and practical phrases emphasizing practical usage. It was a lot of fun taking the class. I think that beginners, indermediates and even native speakers will enjoy it."

             Glen Johnson, Pharm.D., Macon, GA

TABLE OF CONTENTS

Topic	Page #
Introduction	7
Tips for Retention and Objectives	8
Cultural Notes	9
Lesson One – Pronunciation	**11**
Alphabet	11
Vowels	11
Consonants	12
Stress Rules	13
Punctuation Notes	14
Let's Practice	14
Lesson Two – Grammar Part I	**16**
Nouns	16
Adjectives	17
Let's Practice	18 and 23
Pronouns	23
Let's Practice	24
Lesson Three – Grammar Part II	**25**
Verbs	25
First Person Forms	25
Third Person Forms	26
Verb List	27
Let's Practice	29
Verbs with Similar Meanings	29
Let's Practice	31
Using Two Verbs Together	32
The Future	33
Communicating Smoothly in Spanish	33
Let's Practice	34
Lesson Four – The Basics	**35**
Greetings & Courteous Expressions	35
Phrases that Aid in Communication	36
Hispanic Names	38
Numbers and Colors	40
Months, Days, Dates	41

Let's Practice	41
Question Words	42
Telling Time	43
Let's Practice	45

Lesson Five – Pharmacy Vocabulary Part I — **46**

Body Parts	46
Let's Practice	48
Pharmacy Basics	49
Let's Practice	50
Medical Insurance	50
Greeting the Patient and Obtaining Patient Information	51
Asking the Patient to Come Back and Problems with the Prescription	52
Picking-up the Prescription	53
Let's Practice	55
Symptoms and Conditions	55
Follow-up Questions	60
Side Effects	60
Let's Practice and Sample Dialogues	60

Lesson Six – Pharmacy Vocabulary Part II — **63**

Medicine: Drug Routes and Preparations	63
Over-the-Counter and Other Products	64
Let's Practice	65
Prescription Drugs and Drug Categories	66
Drug Allergies	67
Medications the Patient is Currently Taking	67
Let's Practice	68
Directions for Taking Prescriptions	68
Quantity and Frequency	68, 69
How and Why	70
Skipping Doses, Storage, Other Directions	71, 72
Other Descriptions	73
Other Warnings	73
Sample Directions for Use	74
Let's Practice and Sample Dialogues	74
Written Patient Information Reproducibles	77

Conclusion — **79**

INTRODUCTION:

¡Bienvenidos! Welcome to Pharmacy Spanish. Congratulations on your decision to learn Spanish! As you know, the number of Spanish speakers living in the US is increasing rapidly and will continue the uphill trend. By learning Spanish for your profession you are ensuring optimal service to patients.

This program has been customized to teach you only the Spanish you need for your profession. You'll learn vital pronunciation skills to help you speak the language with confidence.

Then you'll learn grammatical formulas that will enable you to put together any necessary phrase or sentence for a variety of pharmacy situations. You will only learn the grammar you need.

Additionally, the program provides some basic terminology, which is good for any situation. This includes: greetings, numbers, days and times. This section will prime you for what's to come. It will also enable you to engage in small talk with any Spanish speaker.

The last two lessons are vital. They contain all of the specific pharmaceutical terminology that you will need. They covers body parts, symptoms, conditions, drugs, allergies, directions for use, insurance information and patient information, among other topics. These lessons contain expressions that are already put together for your use, as well as easy formulas for you to create your own phrases.

To get the full benefit of each lesson, choose a quiet place where you can practice without interruption and choose a time when your mind is fresh. The length of each lesson is roughly one hour, though each can take longer depending upon how much practice you need.

Be sure to utilize the audio (from the mp3 digital audio files, the audio CDs or within the online program itself). Once you've started the program, simply follow my instructions. There will be a pause after a phrase is spoken in Spanish, giving you time to reply. Since you are learning a new language, it is critical that you speak out in a normal conversational voice when you respond. After you reply, you will hear the phrase repeated for reinforcement.

Your active participation is essential for your success in learning this course material.
It is important to note that this is a reference course. You will not learn all of this content in six hours. The teaching portion is meant to orient you to the subject matter. You will learn by continuously practicing the phrases you find most helpful and useful. Practice as often as you can. Perfect practice makes perfect. The more you listen and practice your new language, the more comfortable you will be when communicating in it. Good luck!

¡Buena suerte!

stephanie@handsonspanish.com
Feel free to contact me with questions.

TIPS FOR RETENTION:

This program contains lots of material. In order to increase your retention and learn the content as effectively as possible, we recommend that you follow the tips below.

- Minimize distractions.
- Choose a time when you are alert.
- Study frequently in small increments.
- Utilize the audio (mp3 digital audio, audio CDs or audio in online course) and repeat each phrase out loud as you proceed through the course.
- Identify the phrases you will use the most and commit them to memory.
- Practice frequently.

Course Objectives for Pharmacy Spanish

Introduction:

1. Compare cultural traits of Latinos to those of European Americans.

Lesson 1: Pronunciation

1. Correctly pronounce any word in Spanish.

Lessons 2 and 3: Grammar

1. Communicate in complete sentences.

Lesson 4: Basic Vocabulary

1. Greet a Spanish-speaking patient and ask basic questions.
2. State the date and time.
3. List the components of a Spanish-speaker's full name for correct identification and filing.

Lesson 5: Pharmacy Vocabulary Part I

1. Discuss symptoms and medical conditions.
2. Discuss insurance.
3. Inform patients of prescription status (includes drop-off and pick-up terminology).
4. Communicate problems with refills.

Lesson 6: Pharmacy Vocabulary Part II

1. Obtain personal information, such as drug allergies and current medications.

2. Name prescription and over-the-counter medications.

3. Give accurate directions for use including warnings of side effects and drug interactions.

LA INTRODUCCIÓN -- INTRODUCTION

Objective of the Introduction:
• Compare cultural traits of Latinos to those of European Americans.

DEFINITIONS:

1. "Hispanic" is used to refer to a group of Spanish speakers regardless of country of origin. Spanish speakers do not usually use that term to refer to themselves. A Spaniard, Puerto Rican, Mexican, Venezuelan and Panamanian would all be Hispanic, as would a Spanish speaker living in the US. A Brazilian would not be (as Portuguese is Spoken in Brazil). "Hispanic" is a linguistic term, not a geographical one.

2. "Latino" is a term used to refer to people who live in Latin America (the parts of North and South America south of the US) and does not refer exclusively to Spanish speakers. It does not refer to Spaniards.

CULTURAL NOTES:

This list is only meant to give an overview of the general differences between Spanish speakers of certain cultures and the general traits of English speakers in the US. These traits do not apply to all Spanish-speakers. Simply use them as background knowledge to help in situations where culture may be the reason there is a lack of understanding.

▶ Not all Spanish speakers are Mexican; however, many that you will see at your work will be because of the high percentage of Mexican-Americans in our country (New York has a high percentage of Puerto Rican-Americans and Florida has a high percentage of Cuban-Americans). Overall, about 60% of the Spanish-speakers in the US are of Mexican descent. Never assume the country of origin of a Spanish speaker. Instead, ask,

"**¿De dónde es usted?**"   [day **doan**-day ace oo-**staid**]   "Where are you from?"

▶ There are reasons why your Spanish-speaking patients may not speak as much English as you'd like for them to speak. A lower socio-economic bracket makes up a higher percentage of those who are in the U.S. to work. This translates to a higher illiteracy rate and less emphasis on education. They may be here temporarily. This is one reason that many are not as inclined to learn English and / or may not be literate in Spanish. Also, English is a MUCH more difficult language to learn. Children learn faster and easier than adults.

▶ Family values are very important to Spanish-speakers. It is not uncommon for more than one generation to live together. Also, child-rearing is the responsibility of the whole (extended) family. Traditional values are very important.

▶ You may notice that more than one person comes to drop-off/pick-up a prescription because they support one another. They will often interpret for one another (children are used, as well, to interpret). You shouldn't rely solely on a child's interpretation as a child does not understand healthcare issues or medical terminology.

▶ Trust, honor, respect and loyalty are very important to Spanish speakers. They will typically show you respect for your position of authority, will take you seriously, do as you say and return if you are helpful to them (even if you speak only a little Spanish to them). They will also tell their friends! They are terrific repeat customers and sources for referral customers.

▶ Spanish speakers typically stand closer together when they are speaking. This "inter-personal" distance is sometimes uncomfortable for English speakers. However, if you back up, they may just step forward!

IMPORTANT NOTE: Remember to use the audio (mp3 files from digital audio program, audio CDs or audio in the online course) as you proceed through the program.

Please note that while we stand behind the accuracy of the content, the author of this course shall not be held responsible for any harm which may come from a person's usage of the information within as the production of the language by participants is out of our realm of control.

Lección Uno / Lesson One

LA PRONUNCIACIÓN / PRONUNCIATION

Objective of this lesson:
• Correctly pronounce any word in Spanish.

El Alfabeto Español / The Spanish Alphabet
(in order vertically)

Remember to **use the audio** (mp3 digital audio, audio CDs or audio in online course) as you proceed through the course.

a	h	ñ	u
b	i	o	v
c	j	p	w
ch (one letter)	k	q	x
d	l	r	y
e	ll (one letter)	rr (one letter)	z
f	m	s	
g	n	t	

Is your Spanish pronunciation RED HOT?

Don't worry! It can be with a little help! The good news is that Spanish sounds as it looks. Each vowel has the same pronunciation in every situation. There are only 3 stress rules in Spanish. By contrast, a typical ESOL (English for Speakers of Other Languages) text contains a section on English stress rules which is 35 PAGES long! Once you have learned the sounds and rules presented in this section, you will be able to pronounce ANY WORD IN SPANISH (even the ones whose meanings you do not yet know)!

Las Vocales / Vowels

The key to sounding as authentic as possible is to **keep the vowels short**. Spanish vowels are very choppy; they are never drawn out as in English. This is one reason that Spanish sounds faster than English. In English vowels are sometimes "silent". **In Spanish vowels are always pronounced.**

There is only **one way to pronounce each vowel in Spanish**. Each is always pronounced as follows:

Letter	Sound	Type	Try This:
a	ah	strong	mañana (tomorrow)
e	ay	strong	mes (month)
i	ee	weak	libro (book)
o	oh	strong	dolor (pain)
u	oo	weak	computadora (computer)
y	ee	weak	muy (very)

*Note: "Y" acts both as a vowel and a consonant, like in English.
*Note: Two strong vowels are two separate syllables: mu-se-o
   Otherwise, 2 vowels combine to form one syllable: ciu-dad, vie-jo

Las Consonantes / Consonants

*Consonants with an asterisk have the same sound as in English.

Letter	Sound:	Example:	Pronunciation:
*b	as in English	banana (banana)	bah-**nah**-nah
*c	s (soft) before an "e" or "i"	ciudad (city)	see-oo-**dodd**
	k (hard) before any other vowel	comer (eat)	koh-**mair**
	* "cc" is pronounced "ks"	lección (lesson)	lake-see-**own**
ch	ch	chico (boy)	**chee**-koh
d	softer than in English in the middle or at the end (in some dialects like "th" at middle or end)	dedo (finger)	**day**-doe
*f	as in English	farmacia	far-**mah**-see-ah
g	h (soft) before an "e" or "i" pronounced as the Spanish "j"	gente (people)	**hain**-tay
	g (hard) before other vowels	domingo (Sunday)	doe-**meen**-go
h	always silent	hola (hello)	**oh**-lah
j	h	José (Joseph)	ho-**say**
*k	as in english	kilogramo (kilogram)	kee-lo-**grah**-moe
*l	as in english	luego (later)	loo-**ay**-go
ll	y	Me llamo (I call myself)	may **yah**-moe
*m	as in English	mi (my)	mee

*n	as in English	no (no)	no
ñ	ny	español (Spanish)	ace-pahn-**yole**
*p	as in English	papel (paper)	pah-**pale**
q	k (never kw)	¿Qué? (What?)	kay
r	like "dd" in "ladder"	hablar (to speak)	ah-**blahr**
	trilled /repeated at the beginning of a word or between vowels	para (for)	**pah**-rah / **pad**da
rr	always trilled/repeated	carro (car)	**kah**-row / **cad**do
*s	as in English	sí (yes)	see
t	softer than in English in the middle or at the end	tío (uncle) título (title)	**tee**-oh **tee**-too-low
v	like a "b"	viejo (old)	bee-**ay**-ho
*w	as in English	web (internet)	wabe
x	ks before vowels	examen (exam)	ache-**sah**-main
	s before consonants	extra (extra)	**ace**-trah
*y	as in English	yo (I)	yo
z	s	empezar (to begin)	aim-pay-**sahr**

Las Reglas de Acento / Stress Rules

The "stress" refers to the natural emphasis put on the strongest syllable of a word. For example, "father" is stressed on the first syllable. (**fah**-thur)

In Spanish, there are three simple rules that ALWAYS apply. Use these rules along with the pronunciation guide above to help you pronounce any Spanish word you encounter.

1. If a word ends in a vowel, an "n" or an "s", the natural stress falls on the next to-last syllable.
    Try: **ho**-la, **li**-bros, **ha**-bla, **lla**-mo, me-di-**ci**-na

2. Otherwise, the natural stress falls on the last syllable.
    Try: ciu-**dad**, co-**mer**, ha-**blar**, pa-**pel**

3. Any exceptions to these rules will carry a written accent where the stress should fall.
    Try: **lá**-piz, Jo-**sé**, a-le-**grí**-a

La Puntuación / Punctuation

1. Question marks and exclamation points are also written at the front of a sentence/phrase, but they are upside-down.
   Ex: ¡Hola! ¿Cómo está usted?
2. Accent marks are extremely important in Spanish since they tell us how to pronounce a word, and sometimes even tell us what a word means. For example: **esta** = this, but **está** = is.
   - The accent mark/stress mark is always written the same way: ´
   - Accent marks are written over question words such as "What?" "¿Qué?" or "Who?" "¿Quién?"
   - These words only carry the accent mark when they are used to ask questions, never when they are used to give information.

   Ex: ¿<u>Qué</u> dice la madre?   <u>What</u> does the mother say?
   Ella dice <u>que</u> tiene una hija.   She says <u>that</u> she a daughter.
3. When an accent mark is written over a word with only one syllable, it is to distinguish that word from another without an accent mark.
   Ex: el = the   but   él = he
             si = if   but   sí = yes

¡Practiquemos! / Let's Practice!
Be sure to practice what you have learned before moving on to the next lesson.

Actividad I
For each word below, based on the stress rules you have learned, underline the syllable that would receive the stress/emphasis. Do not look at the next page until you are finished.

1. to-mar
2. me-di-ca-men-to
3. re-ce-ta
4. pa-cien-te
5. tra-gar
6. ha-cer
7. nú-me-ro
8. mé-di-co

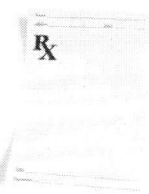

la receta

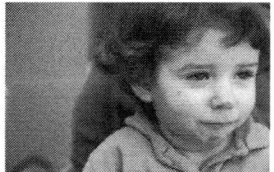

la paciente

Answers:

1. to-**mar** (to take)
2. me-di-ca-**men**-to (medication)
3. re-**ce**-ta (prescription)
4. pa-**cien**-te (patient)
5. tra-**gar** (to swallow)
6. ha-**cer** (to do / to make)
7. **nú**-me-ro (number)
8. **mé**-di-co (doctor/physician)

Activity II

Pronounce each word below. This is an audio activity and should be done while listening to the audio program (mp3 digital audio files, audio CDs or in the online program). As pronunciation rules are different in Spanish, you will pronounce Spanish speaking countries differently in Spanish.

1. tableta (tablet)
2. apetito (appetite)
3. asma (asthma)
4. ibuprofena (ibuprofen)
5. producto (product)
6. minuto (minute)
7. tos (cough)
8. boca (mouth)
9. Argentina
10. Venezuela
11. Chile
12. Colombia
13. Puerto Rico
14. España
15. Perú
16. México **

**Note: In Mexico, due to indigenous pronunciation, the letter "x" is often pronounced "h".

¡Felicidades! Congratulations! You have reached the end of Lesson One!

Lección Dos / Lesson Two
LA GRAMÁTICA – PARTE I / GRAMMAR – PART I

Objective of this lesson:
• Communicate in complete sentences.

LOS SUSTANTIVOS / NOUNS

A noun is a person, place or thing (e.g., pharmacist, pharmacy, prescription). In Spanish, all nouns are either masculine or feminine. This is not to say that "la computadora" is a girl and that "el teléfono" is a boy. Linguistic gender is very different from how we view gender. Liguistic gender was carried into Spanish from Latin. It is a very important part of each noun. The gender of a noun determines the form of any adjective or article that describes it. For example, you will use the article "el" with masculine words and "la" with feminine words. They both mean "the."

- Generally, if a noun ends in the letter -o, it is masculine.
- Generally, if it ends in the letter -a, it is feminine.

Of course, there are exceptions: el agua, la mano, el día, la radio, etc. The safest way to memorize the gender of a noun is to memorize its article ("el" or "la") with it. You can color-code nouns on flash cards to help you remember their gender.

Here are some nouns for you to learn:

Masculine Nouns
el papel (paper)
el bolígrafo (pen)
el libro (book)
el dinero en efectivo (cash)
el cheque (check)
el cupón (coupon)
el lápiz (pencil)
el medicamento (medication)
el seguro (insurance)
el hospital (hospital)
el teléfono (telephone)
el mensaje (message)

Feminine Nouns
la computadora (computer)
la forma / el formulario (form)
la caja (cash register)
la tarjeta de crédito (credit card)
la calculadora (calculator)
la botella (bottle)
la farmacia (pharmacy)
la receta (prescription)
la medicina (medicine)
la droga (drug)
la oficina (office)
la clínica (clinic)

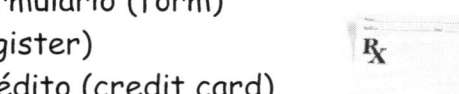
la receta

la medicina

If the noun is a person, the linguistic gender is always the same as the actual physical gender:

el hombre (man) — la mujer (woman)
el chico / el muchacho (boy) — la chica / la muchacha (girl)
el niño (little boy - child) — la niña (little girl - child)
el novio (boyfriend/fianceé) — la novia (girlfriend/fianceé)
el amigo (friend -male) — la amiga (friend- female)
el farmacéutico (male pharmacist) — la farmacéutica (female pharmacist)
el técnico (male technician) — la técnica (female technician)
el doctor (male doctor) — la doctora (female doctor)
el enfermero (male nurse) — la enfermera (female nurse)
el secretario (male secretary) — la secretaria (female secretary)
el esposo / el marido (husband) — la esposa / la mujer (wife)
el padre (father) — la madre (mother)
el hijo (son) — la hija (daughter)
el hermano (brother) — la hermana (sister)
el abuelo (grandfather) — la abuela (grandmother)
el tío (uncle) — la tía (aunt)
el primo (cousin-male) — la prima (cousin-female)
el paciente (patient-male) — la paciente (patient-female)
el cliente (male customer) — la cliente (female customer)

Now that you've learned about the gender of nouns, you must learn the other aspect: number. This one is much easier. All nouns have two forms: **singular** and **plural**.
To make a singular noun plural:

- If the word ends in a vowel, simply add an –s to the end.
  eg: amigo > amigos, farmacia > farmacias
- If the word ends in a consonant, add an -es to the end of the word.
  eg: ciudad (city) > ciudades (cities)

LOS ADJETIVOS / ADJECTIVES

Adjectives are words that describe nouns or pronouns. There are many different types of adjectives: articles, descriptive adjectives, quantitative adjectives and demonstrative adjectives, all of which you'll learn in this section.

All adjectives have one thing in common: **they must all agree in number and in gender with the nouns that they modify.** For example...

- If the noun is masculine and singular, the adjective must be masculine, singular.
- If the noun is feminine and plural, then the adjective must be feminine and plural.

Los Artículos / Articles

Articles are adjectives that always come BEFORE nouns,. This rule applies in both English and Spanish. For example, "the car" is "el carro." All articles (like any other adjective) have four forms: masculine singular, feminine singular, masculine plural and feminine plural.

There are two kinds of articles: **definite** and **indefinite**.

Definite articles refer to specific objects: "el amigo" (the friend). They use definite articles much more frequently in Spanish than we do in English. You've already learned the singular definite articles: **el** and **la**. The plural forms are **los** and **las**. They all mean "**the**."

DEFINITE ARTICLES:

	masculine	feminine
singular	el amigo (the male friend)	la amiga (the female friend)
plural	los amigos (the male friends)	las amigas (the female friends)

¡Practiquemos! / Let's Practice!

Actividad I: Fill in the blank with the correct definite article (correct form of "the").

Options: el   la   los   las

1. _____ recetas
2. _____ medicamentos
3. _____ farmacia
4. _____ dinero

Warning: Answers follow on next page.

Answers:
1. <u>las</u> recetas
2. <u>los</u> medicamentos
3. <u>la</u> farmacia
4. <u>el</u> dinero

la farmacia

Indefinite articles refer to non-specific objects: "un amigo" (a friend). The singular forms mean "a" or "an." The plural forms mean "some." Indefinite articles are: **un, una, unos, unas.**

INDEFINITE ARTICLES:

	masculine	feminine
singular	<u>un</u> amigo (a male friend)	<u>una</u> amiga (a female friend)
plural	<u>unos</u> amigo<u>s</u> (some male friends)	<u>unas</u> amiga<u>s</u> (some female friends)

Los Adjetivos Descriptivos / Descriptive Adjectives

In Spanish, descriptive adjectives almost always come AFTER nouns. For example, "carro nuevo" means "new car." This will seem strange initially, but will feel natural after you become more proficient in the language.

If the adjective ends in the letter -o (masculine singular form), you can change the -o to an -a (feminine singular form). You can add the letter -s to either to make the plural form.

DESCRIPTIVE ADJECTIVES ENDING IN -O:

	masculine	feminine
singular	el amig<u>o</u> simpátic<u>o</u> (the nice male friend)	la amig<u>a</u> simpátic<u>a</u> (the nice female friend)
plural	los amig<u>os</u> simpátic<u>os</u> (the nice male friends)	las amig<u>as</u> simpátic<u>as</u> (the nice female friends)

If the descriptive adjective ends in the letter -e, you will not change the ending to agree with the gender. You can think of the -e as standing for "either." It is gender neutral. You will still need to add an -s to make the plural forms. Examples follow.

DESCRIPTIVE ADJECTIVES ENDING IN -E:

	masculine	feminine
singular	el amigo inteligente (the intelligent male friend)	la amiga inteligente (the intelligent female friend)
plural	los amigos inteligentes (the intelligent male friends)	las amigas inteligentes (the intelligent female friends)

Finally, a few adjectives end in a consonant, not a vowel. Therefore, the form that ends in the consonant is the masculine singular form. This is also the feminine form for some.

Example: joven

For others, just add an -a to the end to make it feminine. If an adjective needs an -a added to it for the feminine form you will see it listed in this course like so: trabajador(a).

Remember: if an adjective ends in a consonant, you have to add an -es to make it plural.

DESCRIPTIVE ADJECTIVES ENDING IN A CONSONANT:

	masculine	feminine
singular	el amigo español (the Spanish male friend)	la amiga española (the Spanish female friend)
plural	los amigos españoles (the Spanish male friends)	las amigas españolas (the Spanish female friends)

Next, you'll find some descriptive adjectives for you to learn. These are all listed as **masculine, singular** (as they are listed in a dictionary). You must change the endings adhering to the rules noted earlier in order to make these adjectives agree with the nouns that you want to describe. In a later section, you'll learn more about when to use these adjectives.

Ejemplos de Adjetivos Descriptivos / Examples of Descriptive Adjectives

PERMANENT CHARACTERISTICS:

grande (big)    pequeño (small)   joven (young)    anciano (old-person)

bueno (good)    malo (bad)   nuevo (new)   viejo (old - object)

alto (tall)    bajo (short)   dulce (sweet)    agrio (sour)

delgado (thin)    gordo (fat)   caro (expensive)    barato (inexpensive)

TEMPORARY CHARACTERISTICS:

sano (healthy)    enfermo (sick)    fuerte (strong) 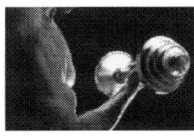   débil (weak)

mejor (better)    peor (worse)   relajado (relaxed)    preocupado (worried)

Los Adjetivos de Cantidad / Quantitative Adjectives

In Spanish, adjectives of quantity always come BEFORE nouns. The most obvious are numbers: **dos** amigos, **tres** amigos, **cuatro** amigos, **cinco** amigos, etc. Numbers just have one form. For example, there is only "cinco" (five). There is no such thing as "cinca, cincos or cincas." The only number that does change forms is the number "one," which we'll discuss later. The most common adjectives of quantity that are not numbers are the words: **mucho and poco.** The singular forms "mucho/mucha" mean "much of " or "a lot of" and "poco/poca" mean " a little of." When they are in their plural forms, "muchos/muchas" mean "many" and "pocos/pocas" mean "few."

QUANTITATIVE ADJECTIVES:

	masculine	feminine
singular	mucho dinero (much money)	mucha comida (a lot of food)
	poco dinero (a little money)	poca comida (a little food)
plural	muchos amigos (many male friends)	muchas amigas (many female friends)
	pocos amigos (few male friends)	pocas amigas (few female friends)

*Note: The masculine plural form can also refer to a mixed gender group.
Example: "Muchos amigos" can refer to a group of male and female friends.

Los Adjetivos Posesivos / Possessive Adjectives

Possessive adjectives come BEFORE nouns. They let us know who owns the object. For example: **mi amigo** = my friend. Possessive adjectives agree with the objects that they describe, not with the people that own the objects. For example: **mis amigos** = my friends. The word "mis" does not imply that I am more than one person; instead, it states that I have more than one friend. The possessive adjectives that you will need to know for your profession are gender neutral; you will not change the endings to agree with the gender of the object described. You will only need to add an -s to describe more than one object. For example, "**su**" can mean "his," her," "your," or "their." It changes to "**sus**" to describe more than one object. Examples follow.

singular	mi amigo (my friend)	
	su amigo (his/her/your/their friend)	"Mi casa es su casa."
plural	mi<u>s</u> amigo<u>s</u> (my friend<u>s</u>)	
	su<u>s</u> amigo<u>s</u> (his/her/your/their friend<u>s</u>)	"Mis casas son sus casas."

If you want to state the <u>name</u> of the person to whom something belongs, you must state possession "the long way around." In English, we use the **'s** as a short-cut. In Spanish, there is no apostrophe-s. To say "Teresa's car," you must say "**el** carro **de** Teresa" (**the** car **of** Teresa). Thus, "Sara's medicine" would be "**la** medicina **de** Sara" (**the** medicine **of** Sara).

¡Practiquemos! / Let's Practice!

Actividad II: Make each subject plural. See the answers at the bottom of the next page.

1. mi amigo español
2. una mujer enferma
3. el hombre inteligente
4. la paciente preocupada

LOS PRONOMBRES / PRONOUNS

Pronouns, such as she, take the place of nouns. They eliminate redundancy. For example: "Mary is my friend. Mary is nice. Mary is tall." sounds awful! Instead, we would say: "Mary is my friend. **She** is nice and tall." In Spanish: "María es mi amiga. **Ella** es simpática y alta." You will only need to learn certain pronouns in order to speak Spanish for your profession. They are all singular.

English	Spanish	Pronunciation
I	yo	yo
you	usted	oo-**staid**
he	él	ale
she	ella	**ay**-yah

"**Yo**" is first person. When speaking of yourself, you use first person. When speaking about others, you use third person. Therefore, "**usted, ella and él**" are all third person. Though usted is technically second person (used when addressing someone), it conjugates like ella and él, so it functions as a third person pronoun.

Caution! Note the accent on "él." If you leave it off, it changes the meaning of the word from " he " to "the."

One more important note about pronouns in Spanish is that you do not have to use them. You should use them if your subject is unclear; however, once the subject is clear, you may omit the pronoun. This is very different from English. For example, in English, you must say, "**He** speaks French. **He** is from France. **He** is tall." You cannot leave off the subject pronouns. In Spanish, however, you can say, " **Él** habla francés. Es de Francia. Es alto." We only used the word "**él**" once. Here's another example: "**Yo** hablo español." and "Hablo español." both mean "**I** speak Spanish," even though the word **I** only appears in the first sentence.

Finally, pronouns are very important. Without them, we would not know how to choose the correct form of the verb to agree with them.

¡Practiquemos! / Let's Practice!

Actividad III: Match each part of speech to a Spanish example of it.

1. sustantivo (noun)
2. artículo definido (definite article)
3. artículo indefinido (indefinite article)
4. adjetivo descriptivo (descriptive adjective)
5. adjetivo de cantidad (quantitative adjective)
6. pronombre (pronoun)
7. adjetivo posesivo (possessive adjective)

a. una
b. inteligente
c. usted
d. pocos
e. mis
f. los
g. chico

Answers to this practice activity:

1.g 2.f 3.a 4.b 5.d 6.c 7.e

Answers to Actividad II (preceding page):
1. mis amigos españoles
2. unas mujeres enfermas
3. los hombres inteligentes
4. las pacientes preocupadas

¡Felicidades! You have reached the end of Lesson Two!

Lección Tres / Lesson Three
LA GRAMÁTICA – PARTE II / GRAMMAR – PART II

Please note that since pharmacy state laws vary, some of the content within this lesson may only be appropriate for Pharmacists. It is important that you adhere to the laws within your state.

Objective of this lesson:
• Communicate in complete sentences.

LOS VERBOS / VERBS

Pronouns, such as he, tell you how to form your verbs. For example, you wouldn't say " I walks to work." The word "walks" is the form that you would use with " he and she. " Nor would I say "I to walk to work." In that sentence, the verb has not even been **conjugated (changed)** at all. It is in its **infinitive** or pure form. To make the verb agree with the subject, we must **conjugate** it **(change** it) into a form that does agree with the subject. Therefore, the correct sentence is "I walk to work."

Examples:

infinitive	conjugated (changed) forms
to walk	I walk, you walk, he/she walks

Los Infinitivos / Infinitives

Spanish has different endings for the different verb forms just like English does. **All** Spanish **infinitives** end in one of the following combinations of letters: **-ar, -er, -ir**. Those endings are the equivalent of saying "to" in English. For example:

"**hablar**" means **to speak**   "**comer**" means **to eat**   "**vivir**" means **to live**

La Primera Persona Singular (yo) / The First Person Singular (I)

We must also learn the form of each verb that we can use with the pronoun "**yo**" (I). This is called the **first person singular** form of the verb. The verb forms that agree with **yo** almost always end in the letter **-o**. Simply take off the **-ar, -er** or **-ir**, and attach an **-o**.

Yo hablo means I speak.   Yo como means I eat.   Yo vivo means I live.

You can also leave off the pronoun "**yo**" and the meaning will remain the same (as if the pronoun were there). This is because the verb **endings** imply the pronouns with which they match. The pronoun is implied in the verb ending. It is still important to know which pronoun you're using so that you choose the correct verb form.

Hablo means I speak.   Como means I eat.   Vivo means I live.

La Tercera Persona Singular (usted, él, ella y "it")
Third Person Singular (you, he, she and it)

Finally, we need to learn the **third person singular** form of the verb. This form is extremely important to learn because it is used with all of the following pronouns: **usted (you), él (he) and ella (she)**. It is also used when the subject of a sentence is **any other singular noun** (not a person). In English, we would use the pronoun "it" to refer to such singular nouns. However, in Spanish, <u>every</u> noun has gender (masculine/feminine). Therefore, in Spanish there is no such single pronoun (e.g., it) when referring to objects. However, you can use this form of the verb to talk about singular objects.

To form the third person singular verb form, simply take off the **-ar** and add an **-a,** or take of the **-er** or **-ir** and add an **-e**. See the examples below, which use the same verbs with different pronouns:

Él habla = He speaks.   Él come = He eats.   Él vive = He lives.
Ella habla = She speaks.   Ella come = She eats.   Ella vive = She lives.
Usted habla = You speak.   Usted come = You eat.   Usted vive = You live.

This is also the verb form that you would use when talking about a single person when using his/her name instead of the pronouns "él" and "ella" (he and she). For example:

Juan habla.   Juan come.   Juan vive.   (Juan speaks, eats & lives.)
Sara habla.   Sara come.   Sara vive.   (Sara speaks, eats & lives.)

LA LISTA DE VERBOS / VERB LIST

Now that you know how to use pronouns and verbs, it is time for you to start building your verb repertoire. The verbs in this section will be most helpful in your profession. You will learn what they mean in English and you will see the infinitive (ending in **-ar, -er & -ir**), the first person singular (conjugated for "**yo**" and ending in **-o**), and the third person singular (conjugated for **él, ella & usted** and ending in **-a** or **-e**). **Irregular forms are noted** with this mark *. You will simply have to memorize these forms since they do not follow the patterns you've learned. Also, some Spanish verbs appear in bold. We will discuss these in the next section. Here is a sample of what you will see in the chart:

English	Infinitive (Span)	1st person	3rd person
to ask	**preguntar**	pregunto	pregunta

**When a verb is in bold, you will see a further explanation in the next section.

English (to…)	Infinitive (Span) (-ar /-er /-ir)	1st person (Yo…)	3rd person (usted, él, ella)
to ask for	**pedir**	* pido	* pide
to be	**estar**	* estoy	* está
to be	**ser**	* soy	* es
to be able to	poder	* puedo	* puede
to breathe	respirar	respiro	respira
to bring	traer	* traigo	trae
to buy	comprar	compro	compra
to call	llamar	llamo	llama
to close	cerrar	* cierro	* cierra
to come	venir	* vengo	* viene
to do / to make	hacer	*hago	hace
to drink	beber	bebo	bebe
to eat	comer	como	come
to explain	explicar	explico	explica
to fill (rx)	surtir	surto	surte
to fill out	llenar	lleno	llena
to follow	seguir	* sigo	* sigue
to give	dar	* doy	da
to go	ir	* voy	* va
to have	tener	* tengo	* tiene
to hear	oír	* oigo	* oye
to hurt	doler	* duelo	* duele
to know	**conocer**	* conozco	conoce
to know	**saber**	* sé	sabe
to leave	salir	* salgo	sale
to listen to	escuchar	escucho	escucha
to live	vivir	vivo	vive
to look at/watch	mirar	miro	mira
to mix	mezclar	mezclo	mezcla

llamar

comer

to need	necesitar	necesito	necesita
to open	abrir	abro	abre
to ought to	deber	debo	debe
to pay	pagar	pago	paga
to pick up	recoger	* recojo	recoge
to prefer	preferir	* prefiero	* prefiere
to prepare	preparar	preparo	prepara
to prescribe	recetar	receto	receta
to put/place	poner	* pongo	pone
to read	leer	leo	lee
to refill	surtir (de nuevo)	surto (de nuevo)	surte (de nuevo)
to repeat	repetir	* repito	* repite
to require	requerir	* requiero	* requiere
to rest	descansar	descanso	descansa
to return	**devolver**	* devuelvo	* devuelve
to return	**regresar**	regreso	regresa
to return	**volver**	* vuelvo	* vuelve
to say/tell	decir	* digo	* dice
to see	ver	* veo	ve
to sell	vender	vendo	vende
to sign	firmar	firmo	firma
to sleep	dormir	* duermo	* duerme
to take	tomar	tomo	toma
to talk/speak	hablar	hablo	habla
to understand	comprender	comprendo	comprende
to use	usar	uso	usa
to wait	esperar	espero	espera
to walk	caminar	camino	camina
to want to	querer	* quiero	*quiere
to work	trabajar	trabajo	trabaja
to write	escribir	escribo	escribe

dormir

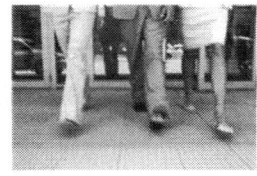

caminar

¡Practiquemos! / Let's Practice!

Actividad I Fill in the missing forms from the verb conjugation chart below. Follow the example (first line). See how many you can recall without looking at the course content. See answers on the next page.

(to...)	(-ar, -er, -ir)	(yo...)	(usted, él, ella)
to breathe	respirar	respiro	respira
	tomar		
	surtir		
	llenar		
	explicar		
	comer		
	pagar		
	comprender		
	usar		
	preparar		

There are a couple of other important verbs for you to learn that do not follow the patterns in the verb list.

The verb **hay** means **there is/there are**. "Hay" only has one form.
  Hay un lápiz. Hay dos lápices.

Also, you should know that "**Me gusta...**" means "**I like...**" (literally, it means "...is pleasing to me).
  Me gusta el libro. (The book is pleasing to me.)

The other form, "**Le gusta...**" means "**He/She/You/ like(s)...**" (literally, it means "...is pleasing to him/her/you).
  A Juan le gusta el libro. (Juan likes the book.)

Los Verbos con Significados Semejantes / Verbs With Similar Meanings

Certain verbs in Spanish have very similar meanings. However, you do need to make a distinction since they are used differently. You can refer back to the verb list as you note these differences:

Ser and **estar**: They both mean "to be." Use "ser" to describe the essence of something/someone. Use "estar" to desribe the state of being of something/someone. In other words, "ser" is used to decribe things that are more permanent and "estar" is used to describe things that are more temporary (like location and temporary conditions). "Ser" has many more uses and you will see examples of them in the rest of this program. In Lesson 2, you learned examples of descriptive adjectives.

PERMANENT CHARACTERISTICS: Use ser with these adjectives.

- grande (big)   /   pequeño (small)
- joven (young)   /   anciano (old-person)
- bueno (good)   /   malo (bad)
- nuevo (new)   /   viejo (old - object)
- alto (tall)   /   bajo (short)
- delgado (thin)   /   gordo (fat)
- dulce (sweet)   /   agrio (sour)
- caro (expensive) /   barato (inexpensive)

TEMPORARY CHARACTERISTICS: Use "estar" with these adjectives.

- sano (healthy)   /   enfermo (sick)
- fuerte (strong)   /   débil (weak)
- mejor (better)   /   peor (worse)
- relajado (relaxed)   /   preocupado (worried)

Answers to Practice Activity I on preceding page:

(to…)	(-ar, -er, -ir)	(yo…)	(usted, él, ella)
to breathe	respirar	respiro	respira
to take	tomar	tomo	toma
to fill (a prescription)	surtir	surto	surte
to fill (out a form)	llenar	lleno	llena
to explain	explicar	explico	explica
to eat	comer	como	come
to pay	pagar	pago	paga
to understand	comprender	comprendo	comprende
to use	usar	uso	usa
to prepare	preparar	preparo	prepara

Saber and **conocer**: They both mean "to know." Use "conocer" when stating that you know (are familiar with) a person or place. Use "saber" when speaking of factual or procedural knowledge.   *****Ella sabe tomar la medicina.** (She knows how to take the medicine.)
   *****Ella conoce a Juan.** (She knows Juan.)

Llenar and **surtir**: They both mean "to fill." However, "llenar" means 'to fill out" as in a form, while "surtir" means "to fill" as in a prescription.
   * **María llena la forma.** (María fills out the form.)
   * **Yo surto la receta**. (I fill the prescription.)

Volver, devolver and **regresar**: They all mean "to return." Use "volver" or "regresar" when speaking of a person returning to a location. Use "devolver" to speak of an object that is being returned for a refund.
   * **Yo vuelvo a casa.** (I return home.)
   * **Pepe devuelve la receta a la farmacia.** (Pepe returns the
       prescription to the pharmacy.)

casa

Preguntar and **pedir**: "Preguntar" means "to ask a question." "Pedir" means "to ask for something (a favor, an object)."
   * **Yo pregunto a la paciente que tipo de seguro médico tiene.**
       (I ask the patient what type of medical insurance she has.)
   * **La paciente pide otro medicamento.**
       (The patient asks for another medication).

seguro médico

¡Practiquemos! / Let's Practice!

Actividad II   Pretend you are describing a patient to another pharmacist or technician. Write "es" next to the adjectives that you would use with "ser" and "está" next to those you would use with "estar." Answers follow at the end of this lesson on page 34.

1. _____ alto.
2. _____ joven.
3. _____ enfermo.
4. _____ débil.
5. _____ delgado.
6. _____ preocupado.

Al Usar Dos Verbos Juntos / Using Two Verbs Together

Your Spanish will sound much more advanced once you are able to combine two verbs. You will also drastically increase the number of things you are able to communicate. You naturally combine verbs in English. For example: "You <u>need to fill</u> out this form." "You <u>should take</u> this medicine with water." "<u>Can</u> you <u>return</u> at 4:00?" When you combine two verbs in Spanish, simply **conjugate (change)** the **first verb** and leave the **second verb** in the **infinitive**. The <u>first verb</u> will almost always be one of the following: **deber, necesitar, poder, querer, tener**. These verbs will help you obtain important information from your patients and will allow you to politely tell them what to do.

(deber)   **Usted <u>debe tomar</u> la medicina tres veces cada día.**
                You <u>should take</u> the medicine three times a (each) day.

la medicina

(necesitar)   **Usted <u>necesita tomar</u> la medicina con agua.**
                You <u>need to take</u> the medicine with water.

(poder)   **¿<u>Puede</u> usted <u>volver</u> a las cuatro?**
                <u>Can</u> you <u>return</u> at four?

(querer)   **Yo <u>quiero explicar</u> a usted esta medicina.**
                I <u>want to explain</u> to you this medicine.

la doctora

(tener)   **Yo <u>tengo que llamar</u> a la doctora.**
                I <u>have to call</u> the doctor.

*When using the verb "tener" with another verb, "que" (pronounced "kay") follows "tener."

The <u>most</u> polite way of <u>making a request</u> in Spanish is to use "**Pudiera...**" [Could you (please)...?] or "**Favor de...**" [Favor of...]. Simply put an infinitive after it. Ex: **¿Pudiera llenar esta forma?** or "**Favor de llenar esta forma.**" (Could you please fill out this form?)

You can also use some very general expressions to express similar sentiments. Again, just add an infinitive. For example:

(es necesario)   **Es necesario tomar toda la medicina.**
                     It is necessary to take all of the medicine.

(es importante)   Es importante no beber el alcohol con esta medicina.
                  It is important to not drink alcohol with this medicine.

(es posible)   ¿Es posible recoger la receta hoy?
                  Is it possible to pick-up the prescription today?

El Futuro / The Future

There is a very easy way to express future plans in Spanish <u>without</u> having to learn the future tense! In fact, you already do this in English. Instead of saying "I will eat at 1:00," we normally say "I'm going to eat at 1:00." The meaning does not change. In Spanish, simply use a form of the verb " ir " (to go), add the preposition "a" (to), and then add ANY VERB IN THE INFINITIVE FORM. Examples follow.

Yo <u>voy a llamar</u> al doctor.   I'm going to call the doctor.
Yo <u>voy a usar</u> la forma genérica.   I'm going to use the generic form.
Yo <u>voy a surtir</u> la receta.   I'm going to fill the prescription.

Ella <u>va a leer</u> las direcciones.   She is going to read the directions.
Él <u>va a pagar</u> con cheque. You are going to pay with a check.
¿Usted <u>va a dar</u> la medicina a su hijo?   Are you going to give the medicine to your son?

Al Comunicarse Sin Problemas en Español
Communicating Smoothly in Spanish

<u>ASKING QUESTIONS IN SPANISH:</u> This is accomplished by intonation and /or simply reversing the order of the subject and verb:
<u>Usted habla</u> español.   <u>You speak</u> Spanish.
¿<u>Habla usted</u> español?   <u>Do you speak</u> Spanish?
    **The helping verb "do" is not needed in Spanish when asking questions.
<u>ANSWERING QUESTIONS IN SPANISH:</u> You can answer with a simple   " Sí " or " No."
You could also begin the sentence with "Sí" or "No" and follow it with the answer.
¿<u>Habla usted</u> español?   <u>Do you speak</u> Spanish?
<u>Sí, hablo</u> español.   <u>Yes, I speak</u> Spanish.
<u>No, no hablo</u> español.   <u>No, I don't speak</u> Spanish.

MAKING A STATEMENT NEGATIVE: Simply put the word "**no**" before the verb.
Note that the word "no" in Spanish is "no," as well as "not."

Hablo español.	I speak Spanish.
No hablo español.	I don't speak Spanish.
Yo tomo la medicina.	I take the medicine.
Yo **no** tomo la medicina.	I don't take the medicine.

¡Practiquemos! / Let's Practice!

Answers to Actividad II
Here are the answers to the previous activity (from page 31):

1. **Es** alto.
2. **Es** joven.
3. **Está** enfermo.
4. **Está** débil.
5. **Es** delgado.
6. **Está** preocupado.

Actividad III Translate each English phrase into Spanish. Attempt each before looking at the answer below it.

1. You should take the medicine with water.

   (Usted) Debe tomar la medicina con agua.

2. Can you return tomorrow?

   ¿Puede (usted) volver (regresar) mañana?

3. It's important to take all of the medicine.

   Es importante tomar toda la medicina.

4. I'm going to call the doctor.

   Voy a llamar al doctor (a la doctora).

5. I have to use the generic form of the medicine.

   Tengo que usar la forma genérica de la medicina.

6. Is it possible to pick-up the prescription at four?

   ¿Es posible recoger la receta a las cuatro?

¡Felicidades! You have reached the end of Lesson Three!

Lección Cuatro / Lesson Four
LO BÁSICO / THE BASICS

> Remember to **use the audio** (mp3 digital audio, audio CDs or audio in online course) as you proceed through the course.

<u>Objectives of this lesson:</u>
• Greet a Spanish-speaking patient and ask basic questions
• State the date and time

Before we get to the very specific pharmaceutical terminology, you must first learn the basics: greetings, courteous phrases, numbers, colors, days, months, how to tell time, how to use question words, etc.

Los Saludos y La Cortesía
Greetings and Courtesy

Here you will find basic greetings and courteous phrases to help you express your polite personality even in Spanish! We've also included some phrases and questions to help you in tight situations! **Be sure to listen to the audio as you proceed through the lesson.**

English	Spanish
Hello!	¡Hola!
What's your name?	¿Cómo se llama usted?
What's his name?	¿Cómo se llama él?
What's her name?	¿Cómo se llama ella?
My name is...	Me llamo...
Pleasure to meet you.	Mucho gusto.
The pleasure is mine.	El gusto es mío.
How are you?	¿Cómo está usted?
How is he?	¿Cómo está él?
How is she?	¿Cómo está ella?
Very well!	¡Muy bien!
So-so.	Así así
Not good, I'm sick.	Muy mal. Estoy enfermo/a.
And you?	¿Y usted?
How old are you/ he/ she?	¿Cuántos años tiene?
How many months old is the baby?	¿Cuántos meses tiene el/la bebé?
I am ___ years old.	Tengo ___ años.

and	y
or	o
Good morning.	Buenos días.
Good afternoon.	Buenas tardes.
Good night.	Buenas noches.
sir / Mr.	señor
m'am / Mrs.	señora
Miss	señorita
please	por favor
Thank you.	Gracias.
You're welcome.	De nada.
I'm sorry.	Lo siento.
Bless you.	Salud.
Is there a problem?	¿Hay un problema?
It's not a problem.	No es un problema.
It doesn't matter.	No importa.
How wonderful!	¡Qué bien!
How awful!	¡Qué lástima!
Careful!	¡Cuidado!
Look! Watch!	¡Mire!
Listen up!	¡Oye!
Help! (in danger)	¡Socorro!
Help me, please. (calm request)	Ayúdeme, por favor.
Of course.	Claro.
One moment.	Un momento.
Without a doubt!	¡Sin duda!
I speak a little Spanish.	Hablo un poco español.
Do you speak English?	¿Habla usted inglés?
Slower, please.	Más despacio, por favor.
Repeat, please.	Repita, por favor.
again	otra vez
What (did you say)?	¿Cómo?
How do you say...?	¿Cómo se dice...?
Write it down, please.	Escríbalo por favor.
What is it?	¿Qué es?
What does it mean?	¿Qué significa?
I don't understand.	No comprendo.
I don't know.	No sé.

Because...	Porque.
Because of ... / Due to...	Debido a...
Excuse me...	Perdón...
Good-bye!	¡ Adiós !
See you later!	¡ Hasta luego !
See you tomorrow!	¡ Hasta mañana !

MÁS BÁSICOS / MORE BASICS

with	con
without	sin
Well...	Pues...
at / to	a
at the / to the (masculine noun)	al (a + el)
of / from	de
of the / from the (masc. noun)	del (a + el)
for	por / para
but	pero
always	siempre
never	nunca
maybe	tal vez
each/every	cada
every time	cada vez
before	antes de
after	después de
here (location)	aquí
there (location)	allí
deodorant	el deoderante
soap	el jabón
toothpaste	la pasta dentífrica
shampoo	el champú
dollar	el dólar
dollars	los dólares
cent(s)	el/los centavo(s)
this	este/a (esto)
these	estos/as
that	ese/a (eso)
those	esos/as

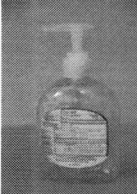
el jabón

la pasta dentífrica

el champú

LOS NOMBRES HISPANOS / HISPANIC NAMES

Spanish speakers typically (but not always) have two last names/surnames. A note that will become important later is that "apellido" is the word for "surname", not for "last name." Though those two mean the same to English speakers, the word "apellido" does not imply last in sequence in Spanish. The first surname (apellido) is from the father (apellido paterno; in example below "**Álvarez**"). The second one is from the mother (apellido materno; in the example below "**González**") **or from the husband** once a female is married.

Forms in the US typically just have one space provided for a surname/last name. A Spanish speaker might read the word "last" and interpret it as last in sequence. This would be "González" in the example that follows (the maternal last name). The problem is that Spanish speakers file things by their paternal surname (the first of the two, or "Álvarez" in the example that follows). You can see how this could cause confusion and how a person could be in your system multiple times.

Next you will find every question you could wish to ask to clarify the name you need. However, we recommend that you use the first phrase in the list, "What is your full name?" in Spanish, "¿Cuál es su nombre completo?". This will get you all components of the name they are using in the correct order. Simply because you now know to file the person below under "A" for "**Álvarez**" doesn't mean that everyone else will. It's best to have as many names as possible.

María	**Teresa**	**Álvarez**	**González.**
Primer Nombre	Segundo Nombre	apellido paterno	apellido materno o del esposo (spouse)

What is your full name?	¿Cuál es su nombre completo?
What is your first name?	¿Cuál es su nombre?
(If you also want a "middle" name)... What is your first name? What is your middle name? What is your middle initial?	¿Cuál es su primer nombre? ¿Cuál es su segundo nombre? ¿Cuál es su segunda inicial?
What is your last name (that you want to file things by)?	¿Cuál es su apellido paterno?
What is your father's last name?	¿Cuál es su apellido paterno?
What are your last names (if you want both – the one they say first is the one you will file them under)?	¿Cuáles son sus apellidos?

What is your maiden name?	¿Cuál es su apellido de soltera?
What name do you go by?	¿Cuál nombre y apellido usa diariamente?
What is the maiden name of your …(family member)?	¿Cuál es el apellido de soltera de su …(family member)?
What is your mother's maiden name?	¿Cuál es el apellido de soltera de su madre?
There is a three name limit.	Solamente se puede poner un nombre y dos apellidos; solamente hay tres espacios.
Is your name spelled correctly here?	¿Es correcto el deletreo de su nombre y sus apellidos aquí?
Is this how you'd like your name to appear?	¿Es como quiere usted que su nombre completo aparezca?
What is the name of your…(family member)?	¿Cómo se llama su…(madre/padre /hijo/hija/, etc.)?
Is this correct?	¿Es correcto?
Are you sure?	¿Está seguro/a?

NAME DIAGRAM

Use the name diagram below to ascertain the proper name from Spanish speakers.

Ella se llama	María	Teresa	Álvarez	González.
	primer nombre	segundo nombre	apellido paterno	apellido materno o del esposo

"Necesito (point to a name above) este nombre / apellido de usted / de él / de ella." "I need (point to a name above) this name from you / from him / from her." (or just "Este")

"Necesito (point to a name above) estos nombres/apellidos de usted/de él/ de ella." "I need (point to a name above) these names from you / from him / from her." (or just "Estos")

LOS NÚMEROS / NUMBERS

1 - 10:   uno, dos, tres, cuatro, cinco, seis, siete, ocho, nueve, diez
11-19:   once, doce, trece, catorce, quince, dieciséis, diecisiete, dieciocho, diecinueve
20-29:   veinte, veintiuno, veintidós, veintitrés, veinticuatro, veinticinco, veintiséis, veintisiete, veintiocho, veintinueve
30-39:   treinta, treinta y uno, treinta y dos, treinta y tres, treinta y cuatro treinta y cinco, treinta y seis, treinta y siete, treinta y ocho, treinta y nueve
40 - 90:   [Follow the pattern for 30-39] cuarenta, cincuenta, sesenta, setenta, ochenta, noventa
100-900:   ciento, doscientos, trescientos, cuatrocientos, quinientos, seiscientos, setecientos, ochocientos, novecientos

1.000	mil	** The decimal and comma are the opposite in Spanish numbers.
2.000	dos mil	
1.000.000	millón	
2.000.000	dos millones	

* "**Hay**" means "there is / there are."

<u>Expressing years:</u>
1999 = mil, novecientos, noventa y nueve
2010 = dos mil diez

<u>Stating how many there are:</u>
There are 33 pills. **Hay treinta y tres píldoras.**

LOS COLORES / COLORS

negro	black
blanco	white
gray	gris
café / marrón	brown
rojo	red
rosa / rosado	pink
amarillo	yellow
verde	green
azul	blue
violeta / morado	violet / purple
anaranjado	orange

LOS MESES/MONTHS beginning with January (Months not capitalized in Spanish)
enero, febrero, marzo, abril, mayo, junio, julio, agosto, septiembre, octubre, noviembre, diciembre

LOS DÍAS / DAYS starting with Monday (not capitalized)
lunes, martes, miércoles, jueves, viernes, sábado, domingo

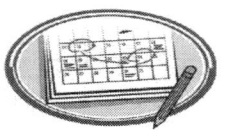

LA FECHA / DATE
Always state the date first (counting number: "dos", "tres"), then the month, then the year: March 15th, 2014 would be **el quince de marzo, dos mil catorce**. Exception: 1st = el primero

¡ Practiquemos ! – Let's Practice !

Actividad I: Fill in each blank with the missing word from the **word bank**. Not all options are used.

por	cincuenta	tres	buenos
buenas	bien	luego	bueno
dice	despacio	enero	llama
llamo	nombre	jueves	setenta y seis
sesenta y siete	violeta	lunes	uno

1. ¿Cómo se_____usted?
2. ¡ Muy _____ ! ¿Y cómo está usted?
3. _____ días.
4. _____ noches.
5. _____ favor
6. Más_____, por favor.
7. ¿Cómo se _____...?
8. ¡ Hasta _____ !
9. ¿Cuál es su _____ completo?
10. Hay _____(50) tabletas.
11. Tengo _____(67) años.
12. La cápsula es rosa y _____.
13. Monday, February 13th would be _____el trece de febrero.
14. Tuesday, January 17th would be martes el diecisiete de _____.
15. Friday, March 3rd would be viernes, el _____ de marzo.

Answers follow on next page.

Answers:
1. ¿Cómo se <u>llama</u> usted?
2. ¡ Muy <u>bien</u> ! ¿Y cómo está usted?
3. <u>Buenos</u> días.
4. <u>Buenas</u> noches.
5. <u>por</u> favor
6. Más <u>despacio</u>, por favor.
7. ¿Cómo se <u>dice</u>...?
8. ¡ Hasta <u>luego</u> !
9. ¿Cuál es su <u>nombre</u> completo?
10. Hay <u>cincuenta</u> (50) tabletas.
11. Tengo <u>sesenta y siete</u>(67) años.
12. La cápsula es rosa y <u>violeta</u>.
13. Monday, February 13th would be <u>lunes</u> el trece de febrero.
14. Tuesday, January 17th would be martes el diecisiete de <u>enero</u>.
15. Friday, March 3rd would be viernes, el <u>tres</u> de marzo.

LAS PREGUNTAS - QUESTION WORDS

These are very important words to learn!! You can use these words alone to get information when you don't have time to ask the entire question.

Who?	¿ Quién ?
What?	¿ Qué ?
When?	¿ Cuándo ?
Where?	¿ Dónde ?
Where is ...?	¿ Dónde está...?
Where's the restroom?	¿ Dónde está el baño / la facilidad?
...OR	¿ Dónde están los servicios/los aseos?
Why?	¿ Por qué ?
Whose?	¿ De quién ?
How?	¿ Cómo ?
Which?	¿ Cuál ?
How much?	¿ Cuánto/a ?
How much is it (does it cost)?	¿ Cuánto cuesta ? OR ¿ Cuánto es?
How many?	¿ Cuántos/as ?
For how long?	¿ Hace cuánto tiempo ?
What time is it?	¿ Qué hora es ?
At what time?	¿ A qué hora ?

¿QUÉ HORA ES?- WHAT TIME IS IT?

Let's answer that last question! When giving the current time, there are certain steps for you to follow:

1. Start your sentence with " **Son las...**," unless you are starting with one o'clock, in which case you would say, " **Es la una.**"
   eg: **Es la una. Son las dos. Son las tres.** ("son las" with all the plural hours)
2. State the **NEAREST** hour.
   - If it is 4:15, you would begin your phrase, " Son las **cuatro**..."
   - if it is 4:45, you would begin your phrase " Son las **cinco**..."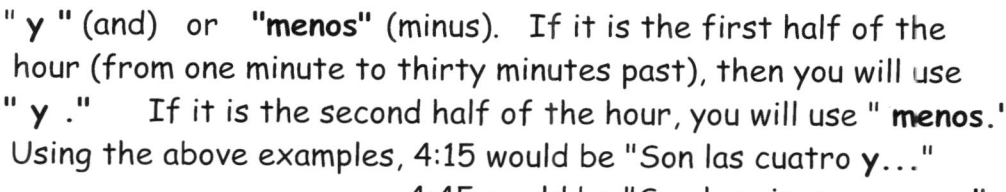
3. Connect the hour and the minutes with either:
   " **y** " (and) or "**menos**" (minus). If it is the first half of the hour (from one minute to thirty minutes past), then you will use " **y** ." If it is the second half of the hour, you will use " **menos**." Using the above examples, 4:15 would be "Son las cuatro **y**..."
   4:45 would be "Son las cinco **menos**..."
4. Next, you need to state the number of minutes either after the hour or before the hour that you stated (the latter will requiere some math!).   4:15 would be "Son las cuatro y **quince**."
   4:45 would be "Son las cinco menos **quince**."
5. Finally, add any descriptive phrases you'd like. You will find these in the list below, along with some other helpful expressions you can use when talking about time.

** Some Spanish speakers will use "para" when subtracting minutes from the next hour and stating the minutes first. For example, instead of "Son las siete menos diez," they might say "Son las diez para siete," which would translate to It's ten till seven or it's ten of seven. Not all Spanish speakers use this system, so it is best to go by the system taught above.

** There is an easier, more casual way of telling time. You can simply state the hour and then add the number of minutes. For example, 4:50 could be stated Son las cuatro y cincuenta.

** Many digital clocks in Spanish speaking countries and many schedules will display military time. At 1:00 p.m., the military time would display 13:00 and so on until 24:00 which is midnight.

<u>English</u>   <u>Spanish</u>
half (30 minutes) past   ...y media (or: y treinta)
quarter (15 minutes) past   ...y cuarto (or: y quince)
quarter (15 minutes) until   ...menos cuarto (or: menos quince)

on the dot	...en punto
a.m.	...de la mañana
p.m. (until ~6:00)	...de la tarde
p.m. (~6:00 until midnight)	...de la noche
midnight	medianoche
noon	mediodía
24 hours	veinticuatro horas
hour(s)	hora(s)
minute(s)	minuto(s)
second(s)	segundo(s)
day	día
night	noche
week	semana
month	mes
season	estación
year	año
now	ahora
later	más tarde / luego
today	hoy
tomorrow	mañana
yesterday	ayer
this weekend	este fin de semana
next weekend	el fin de semana que viene
next...	...que viene
last week	la semana pasada
last...	...pasado/a

In Spanish, they do not say a.m. or p.m. to describe the part of day. Instead, you will choose from: de la mañana, de la tarde, and de la noche. Use de la mañana to talk about any morning hour from midnight to noon. De la tarde refers to the afternoon hours. Depending upon what time supper is eaten in each of the different Spanish speaking countries, de la tarde might be used as late as 10 o'clock. De la noche is used from supper time until midnight.

¿A qué hora? / At what time?

When telling someone **at** what hour something will occur, follow the exact same steps as above and use the same list of expressions to help you. However, instead of beginning your sentence with "Es la..." or "Son las...", you will begin your sentence with "A la..." or "A las..."

Paciente:	Estoy aquí para recoger mi receta.	(I'm here to pick-up my prescription.)
Farmacéutica:	Su receta no está lista.	(It's not ready.)
Paciente:	Pues, ¿qué hora es?	(Well, what time is it?)
Farmacéutica:	Ahora, son las cuatro y veinte.	(Now, it's 4:20.)
Paciente:	¿A qué hora necesito volver?	(At what time do I need to return?)
Farmacéutica:	¿Pudiera volver a las seis menos cuarto?	(Could you please return at 5:45?)

¡Practiquemos! / Let's Practice!

Actividad II: State the time given by each clock.

1.   2.   3.   4.

Answers:
1.) Son las nueve. 2.) Son las cinco. 3.) Son las diez y diez. 4.) Son las cuatro menos cinco.

Actividad III: Match each Spanish question to its appropriate answer.

1. ¿Qué color es?
2. ¿Cómo se llama?
3. ¿Qué hora es?
4. ¿Cuánto es?
5. ¿Dónde está?
6. ¿A qué hora?
7. ¿Cuántas tabletas hay?
8. ¿Cómo está?
9. ¿Habla usted español?

a. Son las cinco y media.
b. Muy bien, gracias.
c. Hay diez.
d. anaranjado
e. Antonio Gómez Lozano
f. A las ocho menos quince.
g. treinta dólares
h. Sí, un poco.
i. en la farmacia

> 1.d 2.e 3.a 4.g 5.i 6.f 7.c 8.b 9.h

¡Felicidades! You have reached the end of Lesson Four!

Lección Cinco / Lesson Five
EL VOCABULARIO FARMACÉUTICO – PARTE I
PHARMACY VOCABULARY - PART I

Please note that since pharmacy state laws vary, some of the content within this lesson may only be appropriate for Pharmacists. It is important that you adhere to the laws within your state.

Objective of this lesson:
- Discuss symptoms and medical conditions
- Discuss insurance
- Inform patients of prescription status
- Communicate problems with refills

The good news is that you will learn the specific terminology for your field in the next two lessons and that many of the Spanish words you will learn look like and sound like the English words. The reason is that most medical terminology comes from Latin. Almost all of Spanish comes from Latin. The bad news is that the next two lessons are the longest, most detailed of the course. There are many types of medicines and symptoms to learn. These lessons are meant to be very comprehensive so that you can use them as a reference.

LAS PARTES DEL CUERPO / BODY PARTS

There are times when patients may speak of parts of the body where they are experiencing pain or discomfort in order to seek your advice about the proper OTC medicine to take. Later, you will learn how to ask which parts hurt, for how long, and what symptoms the patient has. For now, concentrate strictly on the anatomy. This section will be presented so that the Spanish words are in alphabetical order, since the patients will be telling you what parts are causing them problems. This way, you can find the English meaning more quickly. To make these parts plural, simply add an -s (or an -es if the word ends in a consonant).

Spanish	English	Pronunciation
abdomen	abdomen	ab-**doe**-main
amígdalas / anginas	tonsils	ah-**meeg**-dah-lahs / ahn-**he**-nahs
ano	anus	**ah**-no
boca	mouth	**boh**-kah
brazo	arm	**bra**-so
cabeza	head	kah-**bay**-sah
cadera	hip	kah-**day**-rah
canal	urethra	kah-**nall**

cara	face	**kah**-rah
codo	elbow	**koh**-doe
corazón	heart	koh-rah-**soan**
costilla	rib	koh-**stee**-yah
cuello	neck	**k'way**-yo
cuero cabelludo	scalp	**k'way**-row kah-bay-**you**-doe
dedo	finger	**day**-doe
dedo del pie	toe	**day**-doe dale pee-**ay**
diente	tooth	dee-**ain**-tay
encías	gums	ain-**see**-ahs
espalda	back	ace-**pall**-dah
espinilla (de la pierna)	shin	ace-pee-**nee**-ya (day la pee-**air**-nah)
estómago	stomach	ace-**toe**-ma-go
frente	forehead	**frain**-tay
garganta	throat	gar-**gahn**-tah
hígado	liver	**ee**-gah-doe
hombro	shoulder	**oam**-bro
ingle	groin	**een**-glay
labio	lip	**la**-bee-oh
lengua	tongue	**lane**-g'wah
mano	hand	**mah**-no
mejilla(s)	cheek(s)	may-**he**-yahs
miembro	penis	me-**aim**-bro
muela	tooth/molar	**m'way**-lah
muñeca	wrist	moon-**yay**-kah
muslo	thigh	**moose**-lo
nalgas	buttocks	**nall**-gahs
nariz	nose	nah-**reece**
narices	nostrils	nah-**reece**-sace
oído	inner ear	oh-**ee**-doe
ojo	eye	**oh**-ho
oreja	outer ear	oh-**ray**-ha
pantorrilla	calf	pahn-toe-**ree**-yah

pecho	chest	**pay**-choh
pene	penis	**pay**-nay
pie	foot	pee-**ay**
piel	skin	pee-**ale**
pierna	leg	pee-**air**-nah
pulmón	lung	pool-**moan**
recto	rectum	**rake**-toe
riñón	kidney	reen-**yone**
rodilla	knee	row-**dee**-yah
seno	breast	**say**-no
testículos	testicles	tace-**tee**-koo-lohs
tobillo	ankle	toe-**bee**-yo
uretra	urethra	oo-**ray**-trah
vagina	vagina	bah-**he**-nah
vejiga	bladder	bay-**he**-gah
vientre	abdomen (lower)	be-**ain**-tray

¡Practiquemos! / Let's Practice!

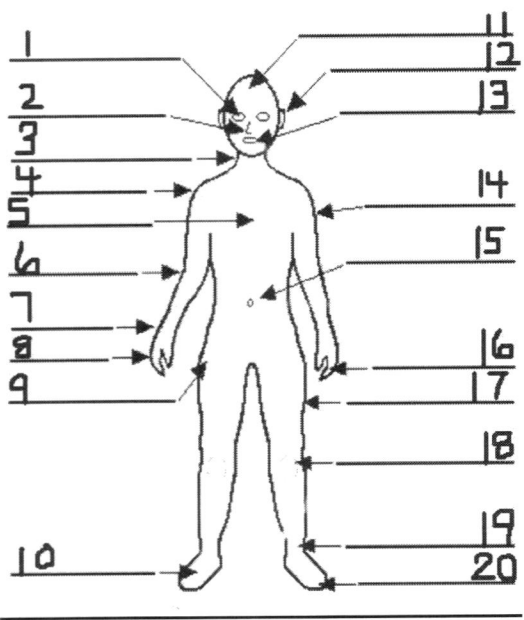

ACTIVIDAD I:
Label these parts using the words below. You may jot down the numbers on a sheet of paper and write the words beside them or you can print this page and label the diagram.

tobillo	**pierna**
brazo	**boca**
pecho	**nariz**
estómago	**cuello**
oreja	**hombro**
codo	**muñeca**
ojo	**cadera**
dedos	**rodilla**
mano	**cabeza**
pie	**dedos del pie**

COMPLETE ACTIVITY BEFORE LOOKING AT NEXT PAGE. ANSWERS FOLLOW.

ANSWERS:

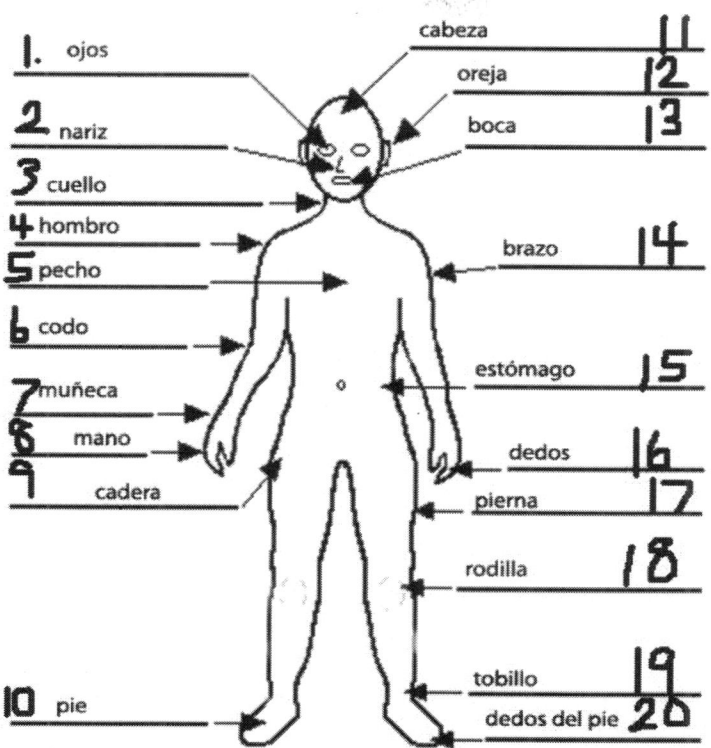

1. ojos
2. nariz
3. cuello
4. hombro
5. pecho
6. codo
7. muñeca
8. mano
9. cadera
10. pie
11. cabeza
12. oreja
13. boca
14. brazo
15. estómago
16. dedos
17. pierna
18. rodilla
19. tobillo
20. dedos del pie

Los Básicos De La Farmacia / Some Rx Basics

You will be learning more about giving directions, warnings, side effects, names of medications, etc. in later sections. First you'll learn very basic information to get you started.

English	Spanish	Pronunciation
bottle	la botella	la bow-**tay**-yah
childproof lid	la tapa a prueba de los niños	la **tah**-pa ah proo-**ay**-bah day lohs **neen**-yohs
easy-open lid	la tapa que abre fácilmente	la **tah**-pa kay **ah**-bray **fah**-seel-**main**-tay
container	el envase	ale ain-**bah**-say
entrance	la entrada	la ain-**trah**-dah
exit	la salida	la sah-**lee**-dah
form	la forma	la **for**-ma
generic drug	la medicina genérica	la may-dee-**see**-nah hay-**nay**-ree-kah
generic form of…	la forma genérica de…	la **for**-ma hay-**nay**-ree-kah day
juice	el jugo	ale **hoo**-go
milk	la leche	la **lay**-chay
label (that you put on the bottle)	la etiqueta	la ay-tee-**kay**-tah

English	Spanish	Pronunciation
name-brand drug	la medicina de marca registrada	la may-dee-**see**-nah day **mar**-kah ray-he-**strah**-dah
new prescription	la receta nueva	la ray-**say**-tah noo-**ay**-bah
refill	el surtido	ale sewer-**tee**-doe
overdose	una dosis excesiva	**oo**-nah **doe**-sees ay-say-**see**-bah
poisoning	un envenenamiento / una intoxicación	oon ain-bay-nay-nah-me-**ain**-toe / **oo**-nah een-**toke**-see-kah-see-**own**
prescription information sheet (about the medicine)	la hoja de información sobre la medicina	la **oh**-ha day een-for-ma-see-**own** so-bray la may-dee-**see**-nah
restroom	el aseo / el baño / las facilidades / los servicios	ale ah-**say**-oh / ale **bahn**-yo / lahs fa-see-lee-**dah**-dace / lohs sair-**bee**-see-ohs
telephone	el teléfono	ale tay-**lay**-fo-no

¡Practiquemos! / Let's Practice!

ACTIVIDAD II: Match each Spanish word to its picture. See the options below the pictures.

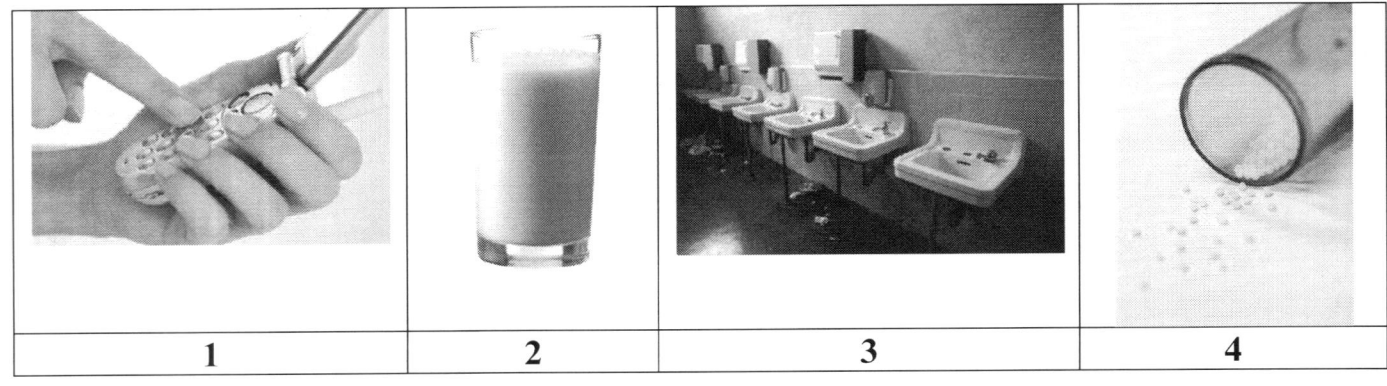

a. la leche   b. el teléfono   c. el envase   d. el baño

ANSWERS:

1.b   2.a   3.d   4.c

El Seguro Médico / Medical Insurance

English	Spanish	Pronunciation
Do you have insurance?	¿Tiene usted... ... seguro médico?	tee-**ay**-nay oo-staid… …say-**goo**-row **may**-dee-koh
I need your insurance card.	Necesito su tarjeta de… ... seguro médico.	nay-say-**see**-toe sue tar-**hay**-tay day… …say-**goo**-row **may**-dee-koh
What type of insurance do you have?	¿Qué tipo de seguro médico tiene?	kay **tee**-po day say-**goo**-row **may**-dee-koh tee-**ay**-nay

What is the policy number?	¿Cuál es el número...	k'wall ace ale **noo**-may-row...
	...de la póliza?	...day la **po**-lee-sah
Your prescription co-pay is _#_ dollars.	Su seguro requiere que usted pague _#_ dólares.	sue say-**goo**-row ray-key-**ay**-ray kay oo-**staid** pah-gay _#_ **doe**-la-race
Any change in your insurance?	¿Algún cambio de seguro médico?	all-**goon** kahm-be-oh day say-**goo**-row **may**-dee-koh
We don't accept this insurance.	No aceptamos este tipo de seguro.	no ah-sape-**tah**-mohs **ay**-stay **tee**-po day say-**goo**-row
The insurance won't cover this drug.	Su seguro médico no paga esta medicina.	sue say-**goo**-row **may**-dee-koh no **pa**-gah **ay**-stah may-dee-**see**-nah
It only pays for the generic.	Solamente paga la...	so-la-**main**-tay **pa**-gah la...
	...forma genérica.	...**for**-ma hay-**nay**-ree-kah
Should we fill it without insurance?	¿Quiere que la surtimos sin seguro?	key-**ay**-ray kay la sewer-**tee**-mohs seen say-**goo**-row
There's a problem with the insurance.	Hay un problema con el seguro.	eye oon pro-**blay**-ma cone ale say-**goo**-row
We're going to call the company.	Vamos a llamar a la compañía de seguro.	**bah**-mohs ah yah-**mar** ah la koam-pahn-**yee**-ah day say-**goo**-row
You need to call the company.	Debe llamar a la compañía de seguro.	**day**-bay yah-**mar** ah la koam-pahn-**yee**-ah day say-**goo**-row

la tarjeta de seguro médico

Al Saludar al Paciente y al Obtener Su Información
Greeting the Patient and Obtaining Patient Information

English	**Spanish**	**Pronunciation**
May I help you?	¿Cómo puedo servirle?	**koh**-mo **p'way**-doe sair-**beer**-lay
Can I help the next person in line?	¿Puedo ayudar a la próxima persona?	**p'way**-doe ah-yoo-**darr** ah la **proke**-see-ma pair-**so**-nah
Have you ever had prescriptions filled here?	¿Hemos surtido sus recetas antes?	**ay**-mohs sewer-**tee**-doe suess ray-**say**-tahs **ahn**-tace
Has the patient ever had prescriptions filled here?	¿Hemos surtido las recetas del paciente antes?	**ay**-mohs sewer-**tee**-doe lahs ray-**say**-tahs dale pa-see-**ain**-tay **ahn**-tace
What is your address?	¿Cuál es su dirección?	k'wall ace sue dee-rake-see-**own**
What is your preferred contact phone number?	¿Cuál es su número de teléfono preferido?	k'wall ace sue **noo**-may-row day tay-**lay**-fo-no pray-fay-**ree**-doe
Do you need help?	¿Necesita ayuda?	nay-say-**see**-tah ah-**yoo**-dah
Let me get that for you.	Lo obtengo para usted.	lo obe-**tain**-go **pa**-rah oo-**staid**
Let me show you where you can find that product.	Voy a mostrarle donde está ese producto.	boy ah moe-**strar**-lay **doan**-day ace-**tah** **ay**-say pro-**dook**-toe

Al Pedir que el Paciente Regrese y Problemas con la Receta
Asking the Patient to Come Back and Problems with the Prescription

English	Spanish	Pronunciation
Calm down, please.	Cálmese, por favor.	**kall**-may-say, pour fah-**bore**
I'm speaking with the doctor.	Estoy hablando con…	ace-**toy** ah-**blahn**-doe cone…
	…el/la doctor/a.	…ale / la doak-**tore** / ah
I have to call the doctor.	Tengo que llamar...	**tain**-go kay yah-**mar**...
	…al / a la doctor/a.	…all / ah la doak-**tore** / ah
We don't have this drug.	No tenemos esta medicina.	no tay-**nay**-mohs **ace**-tah may-dee-**see**-nah
We have to order this drug.	Tenemos que pedir…	tay-**nay**-mohs kay pay-**deer**…
	…esta medicina.	… **ace**-tah may-dee-**see**-nah
It contains the same ingredients.	Contiene los mismos…	cone-tee-**ay**-nay lohs **mees**-mohs…
	…ingredientes.	…een-gray-dee-**ain**-tace
The order comes in ____.	El pedido llega _____.	ale pay-**dee**-doe **yay**-gah
We do not have enough medication to fill your prescription.	Nos falta la cantidad total para surtir su receta.	nohs **fall**-tah la kahn-tee-**dod** toe-**tall** **pa**-rah sewer-**teer** sue ray-**say**-tah.
…We have provided you with	…Le hemos dado	…lay **ay**-mohs **dah**-doe
…(#) pills to hold you over.	…(#) píldoras para ahora.	..**peel**-door-ahs **pa**-rah ah-**oar**-ah
…The balance will be in on (date).	…Tendremos el resto (date)	…tain-**dray**-mohs ale **race**-toe (date)
…You may pay for the medication at that time.	…Puede pagar entonces.	…**p'way**-day pah-**garr** ain-**tone**-sace
When would you like to pick-up	¿Cuándo quiere recoger	**k'wann**-doe key-**ay**-ray ray-koh-**hair**
…your prescription?	…su receta?	…sue ray-**say**-tah
The wait is _#_ minutes.	La espera es _#_ minutos.	la ace-**pay**-rah ace _#_ mee-**noo**-tohs
Can you wait?	¿Puede esperar?	**p'way**-day ace-pay-**rahr**...
Can you wait _#_ minutes?	¿Puede usted esperar...	**p'way**-day oo-**staid** ace-pay-**rahr**...
	…_#_ minutos?	…_#_ me-**noo**-tohs
Can you return in _#_ minutes?	¿Puede usted volver en...	**p'way**-day oo-**staid** bowl-**bare** ain…
	…_#_ minutos?	…_#_ me-**noo**-tohs
Can you return at (time) ?	¿Puede usted volver…	**p'way**-day oo-**staid** bowl-**bare** …
	…a la(s) (hora) ?	….ah la(s) ____(insert time)__
Can you return tomorrow?	¿Puede usted volver mañana?	**p'way**-day oo-**staid** bowl-**bare** mahn-**yah**-nah
You have to call your doctor.	Tiene que llamar a su doctor/a.	tee-**ay**-nay kay yah-**mar** ah sue doak-**tore**/ah
You have to see your doctor.	Tiene que ver a su doctor/a.	tee-**ay**-nay kay bare ah sue doak-**tore** / ah

English	Spanish	Pronunciation
There's only one refill left.	Sólo queda un surtido.	**so**-lo **kay**-da oon sewer-**tee**-doe
The prescription is not ready.	La receta no está lista.	la ray-**say**-tah no ay-**stah lee**-stah
The prescription is ready.	La receta está lista.	la ray-**say**-tah ay-**stah lee**-stah
The prescription will be ready ___date/time___.	La receta va a estar lista ___date/time___.	la ray-**say**-tah bah ah ay-**star lee**-stah ___date/time___.
The prescription is ready for (name).	La receta está lista para…(name)	la ray-**say**-tah ay-**stah lee**-stah **pa**-rah…
We will call you as soon as your prescription is ready.	Le llamaremos tan pronto como su receta esté lista.	lay yah-ma-**ray**-mohs tahn **prone**-toe **koh**-mo sue ray-**say**-tah ay-**stay lee**-stah
We will call you as soon as your prescriptions are ready.	Le llamaremos tan pronto como sus recetas estén listas.	lay yah-ma-**ray**-mohs tahn **prone**-toe **koh**-mo suess ray-**say**-tahs ay-**stain lee**-stahs
Do you need the prescription today?	¿Necesita la receta hoy?	nay-say-**see**-tah la ray-**say**-tah oy
Your prescription has no refills.	Su receta no tiene ningún surtido.	sue ray-**say**-tah no tee-**ay**-nay neen-**goon** sewer-**tee**-doe.
… We are contacting your doctor to obtain refill authorization.	… Llamamos a su doctor para obtener el permiso de surtirla.	…yah-**mah**-mohs ah sue doke-**tore pa**-rah oab-tay-**nair** ale pair-**me**-so day sewer-**teer**-la.
This prescription (medicine) won't	Esta receta (medicina) no va a	**ace**-tah ray-**say**-tah (may-dee-**see**-nah) no bah ah
…have an (adverse) interaction	… tener ninguna interacción	…tay-**nair** neen-**goo**-nah een-tair-ahk-see-**own**
…with your/his/her other	… adversa con sus otras	…ahd-**bare**-sah cone seuss **oh**-trahs
…prescriptions (medicines).	… recetas (medicinas).	… ray-**say**-tahs (may-dee-**see**-nahs)
This prescription (medicine) may	Esta receta (medicina) puede	**ace**-tah ray-**say**-tah (may-dee-**see**-nah) p'**way**-day
…have an (adverse) interaction	… tener una interacción	…tay-**nair oo**-nah een-tair-ahk-see-**own**
…with your/his/her other	… adversa con sus otras recetas	…ahd-**bare**-sah cone seuss **oh**-trahs ray-**say**-tahs
…prescriptions (medicines).	… (medicinas).	…(may-dee-**see**-nahs)
… We are contacting your doctor	… Llamamos a su doctor para	…yah-**mah**-mohs ah sue doke-**tore pa**-rah
…for further instructions.	…más instrucciones.	…mahs een-strook-see-**oh**-nace

Al Recoger la Receta / Picking-up the Prescription

English	Spanish	Pronunciation
The pharmacist needs to speak	El farmacéutico necesita	ale far-ma-**say**-oo-tee-koh nay-say-**see**-tah
…to you about your	… hablar con usted sobre su	…ah-**blar** cone oo-**staid so**-bray sue
… prescription.	… receta.	…ray-**say**-tah

English	Spanish	Pronunciation
...Please step to the Consultation Area...	...Favor de venir a las consultas…	fah-**bore** day bay-**near** ah lahs cone-**sool**-tahs…
... He/she will be right there.	... para esperar a él / ella.	...**pa**-rah ace-pay-**rarr** ah ale / **ay**-yah
Who is the prescription for?	¿Para quién es la receta?	**pa**-rah key-**ain** ace la ray-**say**-tah
Who are the prescriptions for?	¿Para quién son las recetas?	**pa**-rah key-**ain** soan lahs ray-**say**-tahs
What is the name on the prescription?	¿Cuál es el nombre en la receta?	k'wall ace ale **noam**-bray ain la ray-**say**-tah?
What is the prescription number?	¿Cuál es el número de la receta?	k'wall ace ale **noo**-may-row day la ray-**say**-tah
How many prescriptions are you picking up today?	¿Cuántas recetas necesita recoger hoy?	k'**wann**-tahs ray-**say**-tahs nay-say-**see**-tah ray-koh-**hair** oy
Are you picking-up prescriptions for anyone else?	¿Necesita recoger recetas para otra persona?	nay-say-**see**-tah ray-koh-**hair** ray-**say**-tahs pa-rah **oh**-trah pair-**so**-nah
Do you have any questions for the pharmacist about your prescription?	¿Tiene preguntas para el/la farmacéutico/a sobre su receta?	tee-**ay**-nay pray-**goon**-tahs **pa**-rah ale/la far-ma-**say**-oo-tee-koh/kah **so**-bray sue ray-**say**-tah
Next question-- pharmacist only		
Do you have any questions	¿Tiene preguntas	tee-**ay**-nay pray-**goon**-tahs
... about your prescription?	... sobre su receta?	... **so**-bray sue ray-**say**-tah
Do you have any other questions?	¿Tiene más preguntas?	tee-**ay**-nay mahs prey-**goon**-tahs
Please call if you have any other	Favor de llamarnos si tenga	fah-**bore** day yah-**mar**-nohs see **tain**-gah
...questions or	...otras preguntas o	...**oh**-trahs pray-**goon**-tahs oh
... concerns	...preocupaciones	...pray-oh-coo-pah-see-**oh**-nace
...about your prescription.	...sobre su receta.	...**so**-bray sue ray-**say**-tah
Our privacy policy is provided for	Nuestra política de	noo-**ace**-trah po-**lee**-tee-kah day
...you on the back of this	...confidencialidad está al	...cone-fee-dain-see-ah-lee-**dod** ace-**tah** all
...prescription label receipt.	...otro lado de este recibo de la etiqueta de la receta.	...**oh**-troh la-doe day **ace**-tay ray-**see**-bo day la ay-tee-**kay**-tah day la ray-**say**-tah
Please sign (initial)	Favor de firmar (poner sus iniciales)	fah-**bore** day fear-**marr** (po-**nair** suess ee-knee-see-**ah**-lace)
... here to indicate that you	... aquí para demostrar que	... ah-**key pa**-rah day-moe-**strar** kay
... have received it.	...la recibió.	... la ray-see-bee-**oh**
Please sign here to	Favor de firmar aquí para	Fah-**bore** day fear-mar ah-**key pa**-rah
... indicate that you had (did not have)	...indicar / demostrar que (no) tuvo	...een-dee-**car** / day-mo-**strar** kay (no) **too**-boe
...questions for the Pharmacist.	... preguntas para el / la farmacéutico/a.	...pray-**goon**-tahs **pa**-rah ale / lah far-ma-**say**-oo-tee-koh / kah
Did you find everything you werelooking for?	¿Encontró todo bien?	ain-cone-**troh** toe-doe bee-**ain**
Your total is...	Cuesta $$ en total.	k'**wace**-tah $$ ain toe-**tall**
Thank-you for choosing	Gracias por elegir	**grah**-see-ahs pour ay-lay-**hear**

| ...our pharmacy. | ... nuestra farmacia. | ...noo-**ay**-strah far-**ma**-see-ah |
| ...Have a nice day. | ...Qué tenga un buen día. | ...kay **tain**-gah oon b'wayne **dee**-ah |

¡Practiquemos! / Let's Practice!

Actividad III: Indicate whether each phrase would be used when a patient drops-off a prescription (D) or when the patient picks-up (P) a prescription.

1. _____ ¿Cómo puedo servirle?
2. _____ Gracias por elegir nuestra farmacia.
3. _____ ¿Necesita ayuda?
4. _____ Cuesta $$ en total.
5. _____ ¿Puede usted volver mañana?
6. _____ ¡Su receta está lista!
7. _____ Qué tenga un buen día.
8. _____ ¿Cuándo quiere recoger su receta?
9. _____ ¿Hemos surtido sus recetas antes?
10. _____ Favor de firmar aquí para indicar que (no) tuvo preguntas para el farmacéutico.

Answers:

1.D 2.P 3.D 4.P 5.D 6.P 7.P 8.D 9.D 10.P

Los Síntomas y Las Condiciones / Symptoms and Conditions

It's vital that you be able to understand the symptoms that a patient has. This section can be used as a reference when a Spanish-speaking patient lists his/her symptoms for you. You can also use it to determine what to ask of patients.

If a patient gives you information, he/she will use the first person (**yo**) form of the verb. If you ask a patient a question about him or her (or even about someone else), you will use the third person form of the verb (**usted, él, ella**).

*Use estar when discussing the conditions below.

English	Spanish	Pronunciation
I am...	Yo estoy...	yo ace-**toy**...
Are you...?	¿Está usted...?	ace-**tah** oo-**staid**...
Is he/she...?	¿Está él / ella...?	ace-**tah** ale / **ay**-yah...
..pregnant	...embarazada	...aim-bare-ah-**sah**-dah
..breast-feeding	...dándole de pecho	...**don**-doe-lay day **pay**-choh
...contagious	...contagioso/a	...cone-tah-he-**oh**-so / sah
...dizzy	...mareado/a	...ma-ray-**ah**-doe / dah

*Use ser when discussing the condition below.

English	Spanish	Pronunciation
I am hemophilic.	Yo soy hemofílico/a.	yo soy aim-oh-**fee**-lee-koh / kah
Are you hemophilic?	¿Es usted hemofílico/a?	ace oo-**staid** aim-oh-**fee**-lee-koh / kah
Is he/she hemophilic?	¿Es él / ella hemofílico/a?	ace ale / **ay**-yah aim-oh-**fee**-lee-koh / kah

For the rest of the conditions/symptoms that you will need to know, you can use the verb **tener (to have)**. You can simply ask, "**¿Tiene usted/él/ella ...?**" and listen for, "**Yo tengo...**" Here's a sample dialogue to illustrate the use of the extremely important verb **tener**.

Paciente:	Estoy enfermo.	(I'm sick.)
Farm:	¿Tiene usted dolor (pain) de cabeza?	(Do you have a headache?)
Paciente:	No. Tengo dolor del estómago.	(No. I have a stomach ache.)
Farm:	¿Tiene usted la acidez del estómago?	(Do you have heartburn?)
Paciente:	No. Tengo la diarrea.	(No. I have diarrhea.)
Farm:	Usted debe tomar el Immodium A-D ®.	(You should take Immodium A-D®.)

You will ask the patient "**¿Tiene usted...?**" and **fill in the blank with ANY of the symptoms or conditions that follow**. If the person asking is not the patient, you will ask "**¿Tiene ella...?**" or "**¿Tiene él...?**" and **fill in the blank with ANY of the symptoms/conditions in the chart that follows**. The chart is organized by symptom (like symptoms/conditions are grouped together).

If the answer/information comes directly from the patient, **listen for, "(Yo) tengo..."** If it comes from someone else, **listen for, " Ella tiene..." or "Él tiene..."**

- Yo tengo... (I have)
- Él tiene... (He has)
- Ella tiene... (She has)
- ¿Tiene él...? (Does he have?)
- ¿Tiene ella...? (Does she have?)
- ¿Tiene usted... ? (Do you have?)
    ... (fill in with any of the following).

English	Spanish	Pronunciation
...hunger (hungry)	...hambre	**ahm**-bray
...thirst (thirsty)	...sed	said

...sleepy	...sueño	**s'wayne**-yo
...cold (temperature)	...frío	**free**-oh
...hot	...calor	kah-**lore**
...a fever	...fiebre	fee-**ay**-bray
difficulty breathing	dificultad en respirar	dee-fee-cool-**tahd** ain race-pee-**rahr**
difficulty walking	dificultad en caminar	dee-fee-cool-**tahd** ain kah-me-**nahr**
difficulty swallowing	dificultad en tragar	dee-fee-cool-**tahd** ain trah-**gahr**
difficulty seeing	dificultad en ver	dee-fee-cool-**tahd** ain bare
difficulty sleeping	dificultad en dormir	dee-fee-cool-**tahd** ain door-**meer**
fatigue	la fatiga	la fah-**tee**-gah
drowsiness	la somnolencia	la soam-no-**lane**-see-ah
***pain of the/ache in the...	**dolor de...	doe-**lore** day...
...(add ANY body part)	...(add ANY body part)	
headache	dolor de cabeza	doe-**lore** day kah-**bay**-sah
stomach ache	dolor del estómago	doe-**lore** dale ace-**toe**-mah-go
sore throat	dolor de garganta	doe-**lore** day garr-**gahn**-tah
migraine	una migraña	**oo**-nah me-**grahn**-yah
a cramp	un calambre	oon kah-**lahm**-bray
menstrual cramps	dolor menstrual	doe-**lore** main-strew-**all**
nausea	la náusea	la **now**-say-ah
diarhea	diarrea	dee-ah-**ray**-ah
an upset stomach	revuelto el estómago	ray-**b'well**-toe ale ace-**toe**-mah-go
	OR trastorno estomacal	trass-**tore**-no ace-toe-mah-**call**
heartburn	acidez del estómago	ah-see-**dace** dale ace-**toe**-mah-go
indigestion	indigestión	een-dee-hace-tee-**own**
vomiting spells	los vómitos	lohs **bow**-me-tohs
constipation	el estreñimiento	ale ay-strain-yee-me-**ain**-toe
lactose intolerance	la intolerancia a la lactosa	la een-toe-lay-**rahn**-see-ah ah la lack-**toe**-sah
sore throat	dolor de garganta	doe-**lore** day garr-**gahn**-tah
bronchitis	la bronquitis	la broan-**key**-tiece
tonsillitis	la amigdalitis	la ah-meeg-dah-**lee**-tiece
flu	la influenza/la gripe	la een-flu-**ain**-sah / la **gree**-pay
a common cold	un resfriado / un catarro	oon race-free-**ah**-doe / oon kah-**tah**-row
allergy symptoms	los síntomas de alergias	lohs **seen**-toe-mans day ah-**lair**-he-ahs
a cough	una tos	**oo**-nah tohs
congestion	la congestión	la cone-hay-stee-**own**
a runny nose	mocosidad / moquera	moh-koh-see-**dahd** / moh-**kay**-rah
watery eyes	líquido en los ojos	**lee**-key-doe ain lohs **oh**-hohs
dry mouth	una boca seca	**oo**-nah **bow**-kah **say**-kah

coldsores	úlceras en los labios	**ool**-say-rahs ain lohs **la-bee-ohs**
mouth ulcers/canker sores	úlceras en la boca	**ool**-say-rahs ain la **bow**-kah
a virus	un virus	oon **bee**-roose
a bacteria	una bacteria	**oo**-nah bahk-**tay**-ree-ah
a urinary tract infection	una infección del…	**oo**-nah een-fake-see-**own** dale…
	… tracto urinario	…**trahk**-toe oo-ree-**nah**-ree-oh
frequent urination	la orinación frecuente	la oh-ree-nah-see-**own** fray-**k'wayne**-tay
ear infection	una infección del oído	**oo**-nah een-fake-see-**own** dale oh-**ee**-doe
a yeast infection	los hongos	lohs **own**-gohs
dizziness/light-headedness	el mareo	ale ma-**ray**-oh
fainting spells	los desmayos	lohs dace-**my**-ohs
weakness	la debilidad	la day-bee-lee-**dahd**
a sleep disorder	un trastorno del sueño	oon trahs-**tore**-no dale **s'wayne**-yo
weight loss	una pérdida de peso	**oo**-nah **pair**-dee-dah day **pay**-so
weight gain	un aumento de peso	oon ow-**main**-toe day **pay**-so
poor appetite	poco apetito	**po**-koh ah-pay-**tee**-toe
a cut	una cortada	**oo**-nah core-**tah**-dah
a wound	una herida	**oo**-nah air-**ee**-dah
swelling / inflamation	una inflamación	**oo**-nah een-flah-ma-see-**own**
a burn	una quemadura	**oo**-nah kay-ma-**doo**-rah
sunburn	una quemadura de sol	**oo**-nah kay-ma-**doo**-rah day sole
a burning during urination	una quemadura al orinar	**oo**-nah kay-ma-**doo**-rah all oh-ree-**narr**
a bite/sting	una picadura	**oo**-nah pee-kah-**doo**-rah
an itch	una picazón	**oo**-nah pee-kah-**soan**
poison ivy	la hiedra venenosa	la **yay**-drah bay-nay-**no**-sah
jock itch	la tiña inguinal	la **teen**-ya een-guee-**nall**
athlete's foot	el pie de atleta	ale **pee**-ay day at-**lay**-tah
a callus	un callo	oon **kah**-yo
a blister	una ampolla	**oo**-nah ahm-**poe**-yah
acne	el acne	ale **ahk**-nay
a rash	una erupción	**oo**-nah ay-roop-see-**own**
chicken pox	la varicela	la ba-ree-**say**-la
asthma	la asma	la **ahs**-ma
angina	la angina	la ahn-**he**-nah
glaucoma	el glaucoma	ale gla-ow-**koe**-ma
cataract	la catarata	la kah-tah-**rah**-tah
blurred vision	la visión nublada	la bee-see-**own** noo-**blah**-dah
epilepsy	la epilepsia	la ay-pee-**lape**-see-ah
ulcers	úlceras	**ool**-say-rahs

a cyst	una quiste	**oo**-nah **key**-stay
cancer	el cáncer	ale **kahn**-sair
AIDS	la SIDA	la **see**-dah
arthritis	la artritis	la are-**tree**-tiece
dysentery	la disentería	la dee-sane-tay-**ree**-ah
ADHD	el trastorno de hiperactividad y un déficit de atención	ale trass-**tore**-no day ee-pair-ahk-tee-bee-**dod**ee oon **day**-fee-seat day ah-tain-see-**own**
hepatitis	la hepatitis	la ay-pa-**tee**-tiece
anemia	la anemia	la ah-**nay**-me-ah
meningitis	la meningitis	la may-nane-**he**-tiece
whooping cough	una tos ferina	**oo**-nah tohs fay-**ree**-nah
diabetes	las diabetes	lahs dee-ah-**bay**-tace
a blood clot	un coágulo	oon koh-**ah**-goo-low
high cholesterol	un nivel alto de colesterol	oon nee-**bail all**-toe day koh-lace-tay-**role**
high blood pressure	hipertensión /	ee-pair-tain-see-**own** /
	...alta presión arterial	...**all**-tah pray-see-**own** are-tay-ree-**all**
low blood pressure	hipotensión /	ee-po-tain-see-**own** /
	...baja presión arterial	...**ba**-ha pray-see-**own** are-tay-ree-**all**
a heart condition	una condición del corazón	**oo**-nah cone-dee-see-**own** dale koh-rah-**soan**
a pacemaker	un marcapaso	oon marr-kah-**pah**-so
a thyroid condition	una condición del tiroideo	**oo**-nah cone-dee-see-**own** dale tee-roy-**day**-oh
a prostate condition	una condición de la próstata	**oo**-nah cone-dee-see-**own** day la **pro**-stah-tah
a respiratory condition	una condición...	**oo**-nah cone-dee-see-**own**...
	...respiratoria	...race-pee-rah-**toe**-ree-ah
kidney disease	la enfermedad de los riñones	la ain-fair-may-**dod** day lohs reen-**yo**-nace
lung disease	la enfermedad de los pulmones	la ain-fair-may-**dod** day lohs pool-**moan**-ace
pneumonia	la pulmonía	la pool-mo-**nee**-ah
Alzheimer's disease	la enfermedad de Alzheimer	la ain-fair-may-**dod** day all-sigh-**mare**
heart disease	la enfermedad del corazón	la ain-fair-may-**dod** dale koh-rah-**soan**
STD	la enfermedad de…	la ain-fair-may-**dod** day…
	…transmisión sexual	…trahns-me-see-**own** sake-sue-**all**
venereal disease	la enfermedad venérea	la ain-fair-may-**dod** bay-**nay**-ray-ah
liver disease	la enfermedad del hígado	la ain-fair-may-**dod** dale **ee**-gah-doe

** "dolor de..." means "a pain/ache in/of the..." **"Tengo dolor de cabeza,"** then, means "I have a headache/I have a pain in my head." Sometimes you will hear this instead: **"Me duele la cabeza,"** which means, "My head hurts." They both have the same meaning.

Más Preguntas para el Paciente / Follow-up Questions

Some follow-up phrases for you once you determine a patient's symptoms are:

English	Spanish	Pronunciation
For how long?	¿Hace cuánto tiempo?	**ah**-say **k'wann**-toe tee-**aim**-poe
Is this the first time?	¿Es la primera vez?	ace la pre-**may**-rah base
When was the last time?	¿Cuándo fue la última vez?	**k'wann**-doe f'way la **ool**-tee-ma-base
You should see your doctor.	Debe ver a su doctor/a.	**day**-bay bare ah sue doke-**tore**/ah
You should go to the hospital.	Debe ir al hospital.	**day**-bay ear all ose-pee-**tall**
Call 911 !	¡ Llame nueve, uno, uno!	**ya**-may noo-**ay**-bay **oo**-no **oo**-no
You should take...(name medicine).	Debe tomar...	**day**-bay toe-**marr**...
Have you taken ____?	¿Ha tomado___?	ah toe-**mah**-doe...

Los Efectos Adversos / Side Effects

Now that you know conditions and symptoms in Spanish, it will be easy to tell your patients about **side effects** of any medication. Simply skim through the list to see which symptoms might be possible, and say, **" Esta medicina puede causar..."** (This medicine could cause...). Then, you will simply **fill in the blank with ANY symptom from the list above.** For example, **"Esta medicina puede causar dolor de cabeza."**

¡Practiquemos! / Let's Practice!

Actividad IV: Complete the name of each symptom using a word/phrase from both columns.

1. dificultad
2. dolor
3. poco
4. una quemadura
5. el pie
6. la visión
7. el trastorno de hiperactividad
8. una tos
9. alta presión
10. una condición

a. del corazón
b. de sol
c. en respirar
d. ferina
e. y un déficit de atención
f. arterial
g. de atleta
h. de cabeza
i. nublada
j. apetito

(Answers next page...)

ANSWERS:

1.c 2.h 3.j 4.b 5.g 6.i 7.e 8.d 9.f 10.a

Actividad V: Translate the following symptoms into English. Assume the patient is female. Remember that "tiene" means "he/she has" or "you have."

Tiene sed.	
Tiene dificultad en dormir.	
Tiene dolor de cabeza.	
Tiene dolor de garganta.	
Tiene acidez del estómago.	
Tiene la gripe.	
Tiene un resfriado.	
Tiene una tos.	
Tiene la congestión.	
Tiene una infección del oído.	
Tiene el mareo.	
Tiene una cortada.	
Tiene una quemadura de sol.	
Tiene la varicela.	
Tiene la asma.	
Tiene diabetes.	
Tiene hipertensión.	
Tiene un nivel alto de colesterol.	
Tiene una condición del corazón.	
Tiene la pulmonía.	

(Answers next page...)

Answers:

Tiene sed.	She's thirsty. (She has thirst).
Tiene dificultad en dormir.	She has difficulty sleeping.
Tiene dolor de cabeza.	She has a headache.
Tiene dolor de garganta.	She has a sore throat.
Tiene acidez del estómago.	She has heartburn.
Tiene la gripe.	She has the flu.
Tiene un resfriado.	She has a cold.
Tiene una tos.	She has a cough.
Tiene la congestión.	She is congested. (She has congestion.)
Tiene una infección del oído.	She has an ear infection.
Tiene el mareo.	She is dizzy. (She has light-headedness.)
Tiene una cortada.	She has a cut.
Tiene una quemadura de sol.	She has a sunburn.
Tiene la varicela.	She has chicken pox.
Tiene la asma.	She has asthma.
Tiene diabetes.	She has diabetes.
Tiene hipertensión.	She has high blood pressure.
Tiene un nivel alto de colesterol.	She has high cholesterol.
Tiene una condición del corazón.	She has a heart condition.
Tiene la pulmonía.	She has pneumonia.

Actividad VI: Sample Dialogues

- In this exercise, you will be prompted for the Pharmacist's responses to the patient's questions and statements. (**You will need to listen to the digital audio mp3s, the audio CDs or the audio in the online program for this exercise.**)

- This is an oral exercise that pulls together the information from this lesson and gives you real-life scenarios for practice. You will not have a written guide for this portion. It is meant to mimic a real-life scenario in which you are speaking with a Spanish-speaking patient. Try to do this exercise without writing down anything. If you need to hear something again, simply rewind this audio and play it again. After all, in real life, you can say, "Repita, por favor" or "Otra vez."

¡Felicidades! You have reached the end of Lesson Five!

Lección Seis / Lesson Six
EL VOCABULARIO FARMACÉUTICO – PARTE II
PHARMACY VOCABULARY - PART II

Objective of this lesson:
- Obtain personal information such as drug allergies and current medications
- Name prescription & over-the-counter medications
- Give accurate directions for use including warnings of side effects and drug interactions

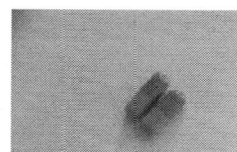 Please note that since pharmacy state laws vary, some of the content within this lesson may only be appropriate for Pharmacists. It is important to adhere to the laws within your state.

La Medicina / Medicine

In this section you'll learn the Spanish names of medications. First you will learn the drug preparations/routes. Next, it will be helpful to learn how to say the different types of over-the-counter medicine. If you do not see one listed, it is because it is referred to by the brand name (the same as the English brand name). You can also use some of these when talking about prescriptions.

Preparación de los Medicamentos / Drug Routes and Preparations

English	Spanish	Pronunciation
oral	oral	oh-**rahl**
orally	por boca	pour **bow**-kah
rectally	rectalmente	rake-tall-**main**-tay
topical	tópica	**toe**-pee-kah
vaginal	vaginal	bah-he-**nall**
vaginally	vaginalmente	bah-he-nall-**main**-tay
capsule	una cápsula	**oo**-nah **cop**-sue-la
cream	una pomada / una crema	**oo**-nah poe-**ma**-dah / **oo**-nah **cray**-ma
drops	unas gotas	**oo**-nahs **go**-tahs
elixir	un elixir	oon ay-**leak**-sair
injection	una inyección	**oo**-nah een-yake-see-**own**
inhaler	un inhalador	oon een-ah-la-**door**
liquid	una líquida	**oo**-nah **lee**-key-dah
lotion	una loción	**oo**-nah lo-see-**own**
lozenge	una pastilla	**oo**-nah pa-**stee**-yah

nose drops	unas gotas para la nariz	**oo**-nahs **go**-tahs **pa**-rah la nah-**reece**
pill	una píldora	**oo**-nah **peel**-doe-rah
powder	un polvo	oon **pole**-bow
spray	un atomizador	oon ah-toe-me-sah-**door**
suppository	un supositorio	oon sue-poe-see-**toe**-ree-oh
suspension	una suspensión	**oo**-nah sue-spain-see-**own**
syrup	un jarabe	oon ha-**rah**-bay
tablet	una tableta	**oo**-nah tah-**blay**-tah

La Medicina que No Necesita Receta y Otros Productos
Over-the-Counter and Other Products

English	Spanish	Pronunciation
thermometer	el termómetro	ale tare-**moe**-may-troh
cough syrup	el jarabe para la tos	ale ha-**rah**-bay **pa**-rah la tohs
cough drops	las pastillas para la tos	lahs pa-**stee**-yahs **pa**-rah la tohs
nose drops	unas gotas para la nariz	**oo**-nahs **go**-tahs **pa**-rah la nah-**reece**
ibuprofen	la ibuprofena	la ee-boo-pro-**fay**-nah
tylenol®	el tylenol ®	ale tee-lay-**nole**
acetaminophen	el acetaminofén	ale ah-say-tah-me-no-**fane**
aspirin	la aspirina	la ah-spee-**ree**-nah
cotton	el algodón	ale all-go-**doan**
bandage	un vendaje	oon bane-**dah**-hay
band-aid ®	una curita	**oo**-nah koo-**ree**-tah
tape	el esparadrapo	ale ace-pa-rah-**drah**-poe
antihistamine	el antihistamínico	ale ahn-tee-ees-tah-**me**-nee-koh
pseudophedrine	la seudofedrina	la say-oo-doe-fay-**dree**-nah
decongestant	el descongestionante	ale dace-cone-hay-stee-oh-**nahn**-tay
appetite suppressant	el supresor del apetito	ale sue-pray-**sore** dale ah-pay-**tee**-toe
sleeping pill	una medicina somnífera	**oo**-nah may-dee-**see**-nah soam-**nee**-fay-rah
vitamins	las vitaminas	lahs bee-tah-**me**-nahs
antacid	el antiácido	ale ahn-tee-**ah**-see-doe
oil	el aceite	ale ah-**say**-tay
ointment	el ungüento	ale oon-**g'wayne**-toe
calamine lotion	la crema de calamina	la **cray**-ma day kah-la-**me**-nah
hydrocortisone	la hidrocortisona	la ee-droh-core-tee-**so**-nah
hydrogen peroxide	el peróxido de hidrógeno	ale pay-**roke**-see-doe day ee-**droh**-hay-no
rubbing alcohol	el alcohol para fricciones	ale all-koh-**ole pa**-rah freak-see-**oh**-nace
contraceptive	un contraceptivo	oon cone-trah-sape-**tee**-bow
condom	un condón	oon cone-**doan**

¡Practiquemos! / Let's Practice!

Actividad I: Label each OTC item in Spanish. Use the word bank below.

las vitaminas	el peróxido de hidrógeno	el jarabe para la tos	el vendaje	las gotas para la nariz
el algodón	las curitas	el termómetro	el ungüento	el esparadrapo

1.
2.
3.
4.
5.
6.
7.
8.
9.
10.

Answers at right:

1. el ungüento	6. el jarabe para la tos
2. el esparadrapo	7. el algodón
3. las vitaminas	8. el peróxido de hidrógeno
4. el termómetro	9. las gotas para la nariz
5. el vendaje	10. las curitas

Medicamentos que Necesitan una Receta y las Categorías de Medicamentos
Prescription Drugs and Drug Categories

English	Spanish	Pronunciation
albuterol	el albuterol	ale all-boo-tay-**role**
ampicillin	la ampicilina	la ahm-pee-see-**lee**-nah
analgesics	los analgésicos	lohs ah-nall-**hay**-see-kohs
anesthetics	los anestésicos	lohs ah-nace-**tay**-see-kohs
amphetamine	la anfetamina	la ahn-fay-tah-**me**-nah
antacids	los antiácidos	lohs ahn-tee-**ah**-see-dohs
antibiotics	los antibióticos	lohs ahn-tee-bee-**oh**-tee-kohs
anticonvulsants	los anticonvulsivos	lohs ahn-tee-cone-bool-**see**-bohs
antidepressants	los antidepresivos	lohs ahn-tee-day-pray-**see**-bohs
antimalarics	los antimaláricos	lohs ahn-tee-ma-**la**-ree-kohs
antiseptics	los antisépticos	lohs ahn-tee-**sape**-tee-kohs
astringents	los astringentes	lohs ah-streen-**hane**-tace
caffeine	la cafeína	la kah-fay-**ee**-nah
cathartics	los catárticos	lohs kah-**tar**-tee-kohs
decongestants	los descongestionantes	lohs dace-cone-hay-stee-oh-**nahn**-tace
diuretics	los diuréticos	lohs dee-oo-**ray**-tee-kohs
emetics	los eméticos	lohs ay-**may**-tee-kohs
emollients	los emolientes	lohs ay-mo-lee-**ain**-tace
estrogen	el estrógeno	ale ace-**trow**-hay-no
steroids	los esteroides	lohs ace-tay-**roy**-dace
phenobarbital	el fenobarbital	ale fay-no-bar-bee-**tall**
insulin	la insulina	la een-sue-**lee**-nah
laxatives	los laxantes	lohs lax-**ahn**-tace
medications for diabetes	los medicamentos para…	lohs may-dee-kah-**main**-tohs **pa**-rah
	…diabetes	…dee-ah-**bay**-tace
narcotics	los narcóticos	lohs nar-**koh**-tee-kohs
penicillin	la penicilina	la pay-nee-see-**lee**-nah
birth control pills	las píldoras	lahs **peel**-door-ahs
	…anticonceptivas	…ahn-tee-cone-sape-**tee**-bahs
purgatives	los purgantes	lohs pour-**gahn**-tace
sedatives	los sedantes	lohs say-**dahn**-tace
stimulants	los estimulantes	lohs ace-tee-moo-**lahn**-tace
thyroid pills	los medicamentos para	lohs may-dee-kah-**main**-tohs **pa**-rah
	…tiroide	tee-**roy**-day
tranquilizers	los tranquilizantes	lohs trahn-key-lee-**sahn**-tace

Note: As you can see, most prescription medications go by the same name in English and Spanish. There are many that do not appear on this list because they are called in Spanish by the same brand name that they are in English. When using a generic, you can say, "la forma genérica de _____" (the generic form of _____) to clarify.

Las Alergias a Medicinas / Drug Allergies

To find out if a patient has a drug allergy, you can use the questions below:

Do you (does he/she) have drug allergies?	¿Tiene (usted / él / ella) alergias a medicinas?	tee-**ay**-nay (oo-**staid** / ale / **ay**-yah) ah-**lair**-he-ahs ah may-dee-**see**-nahs
To which ones?	¿A cuáles?	ah k'**wah**-lace
OR	OR	
Are you (is he/she) allergic to any medicine?	¿Es (usted / él / ella) alérgico/a a cualquier medicina?	ace (oo-**staid** / ale / **ay**-yah) ah-**lare**-he-koh/kah ah k'wall-key-**air** may-dee-**see**-nah
Are you (is he/she) allergic to ____ (fill in the blank with medicine)?	¿Es (usted / él / ella) alérgico/a a _____(fill in the blank with medicine)?	ace (oo-**staid** / ale / **ay**-yah) ah-**lare**-he-koh/kah ah_____ (fill in the blank with medicine)
Example: Are you (is he/she) allergic to penicillin?	Example: ¿Es (usted / él / ella) alérgico/a a la penicilina?	Example: ace (oo-**staid** / ale / **ay**-yah) ah-**lare**-he-koh/kah ah la pay-nee-see-**lee**-nah

Las Medicinas que el/la Paciente Está Tomando
Medications the Patient is Currently Taking

To find out which medications a patient is currently taking, you can use the questions below:

What medicines are you currently taking?	¿Cuáles medicinas está tomando (usted / él / ella)?	k'**wah**-lace may-dee-**see**-nahs ace-**tah** toe-**mahn**-doe (oo-**staid** / ale / **ay**-yah)
What prescription medicines are you currently taking?	¿Cuáles medicinas que requieren una receta está tomando (usted / él / ella)?	k'**wah**-lace may-dee-**see**-nahs kay ray-key-**air**-ain **oo**-nah ray-**say**-ah ace-**tah** toe-**mahn**-doe (oo-**staid** / ale / **ay**-yah)
What over-the-counter medicines are you currently taking?	¿Cuáles medicinas que no requieren una receta está tomando (usted / él / ella)?	k'**wah**-lace may-dee-**see**-nahs kay no ray-key-**air**-ain **oo**-nah ray-**say**-ah ace-**tah** toe-**mahn**-doe (oo-**staid** / ale / **ay**-yah)

¡Practiquemos! / Let's Practice!

Actividad II: Match the Spanish medications and OTC products to their English meanings.

1. unas gotas
2. una pastilla
3. un jarabe
4. un vendaje
5. una curita
6. el aceite
7. el ungüento
8. una medicina somnífera
9. los esteroides
10. una pomada

a. bandage
b. cream
c. oil
d. lozenge
e. steroids
f. band-aid ®
g. drops
h. syrup
i. sleeping pill
j. ointment

Answers: 1.g 2.d 3.h 4.a 5.f 6.c 7.j 8.i 9.e 10.b

Direcciones para Tomar las Recetas / Directions for Taking Prescriptions

When advising patients on how to take medication, simply say, "Tome usted..." or just "Tome..." and **fill in the blanks with quantity and frequency, telling them when and how to take it** (use expressions in the next few sections and make any necessary modifications using what you have learned so far).

Tome...   Take...

You will first need to tell the patient **HOW MUCH** to take:

La Cantidad / Quantity

English	Spanish	Pronunciation
one ounce	una onza	**oo**-nah **own**-sah
two ounces, etc.	dos onzas	dohs **own**-sahs
...and a half	...y media	...ee **may**-dee-ah
a fourth of...	un cuarto de...	oon **k'warr**-toe day...
a third of...	una tercera de...	**oo**-nah tare-**say**-rah day...
a half of...	la mitad de...	la me-**todd** day
one tablespoon	una cucharada	**oo**-nah koo-cha-**rah**-dah
two tablespoons	dos cucharadas	dohs koo-chah-**rah**-dahs

one teaspoon	una cucharita **	**oo**-nah koo-cha-**ree**-tah
two teaspoons	dos cucharitas	dohs koo-cha-**ree**-tahs
one drop	una gota	**oo**-nah **go**-tah
two drops	dos gotas	dohs **go**-tahs
one dropperful	un gotero lleno	oon go-**tay**-row **yay**-no
two droppers full	dos goteros llenos	dohs go-**tay**-rohs **yay**-nohs
one applicator full	un aplicador lleno	oon ah-plee-kah-**door yay**-no
two applicators full	dos aplicadores llenos	dohs ah-plee-kah-**door**-ace **yay**-nohs
a liter	un litro	oon **lee**-troh
a milliliter	un mililitro	oon me-lee-**lee**-troh
a gram	un gramo	oon **grah**-moe
a milligram	un miligramo	oon me-lee-**grah**-moe
¼ tablet	un cuarto de tableta	oon **k'warr**-toe day tah-**blay**-tah
½ tablet	una mitad de tableta	**oo**-nah me-**todd** day tah-**blay**-tah
one tablet	una tableta	**oo**-nah tah-**blay**-tah
two tablets	dos tabletas	dohs tah-**blay**-tahs
one pill	una píldora	**oo**-nah **peel**-door-ah
two pills	dos píldoras	dohs **peel**-door-ahs
one capsule	una cápsula	**oo**-nah **cop**-sue-lah
two capsules	dos cápsulas	dohs **cop**-sue-lahs

** Some say "cucharadita" [pronounced: koo-chah-rah-**dee**-tah]. Both are correct.

Next, you will need to tell the patient WHEN to take the medicine:
La Frecuencia / Frequency

English	Spanish	Pronunciation
once daily	una vez al día	**oo**-nah base all **dee**-ah
twice daily	dos veces al día	dohs **bay**-sace all **dee**-ah
three times daily	tres veces al día	trace **bay**-sace all **dee**-ah
# times a day	#_ veces al día	#_ **bay**-sace all **dee**-ah
every other day / every two days	cada dos días	**kah**-dah dohs **dee**-ahs
once weekly / once a week	una vez a la semana	**oo**-nah base ah la say-**ma**-nah
twice weekly / twice a week	dos veces a la semana	dohs **bay**-sace ah la say-**ma**-nah
# times a week	#_ veces a la semana	#_ **bay**-sace ah la say-**ma**-nah
until gone	hasta que no hay más	**ah**-stah kay no eye mahs
every #_ hours	cada #_ horas	**kah**-dah #_ **oh**-rahs
every four hours	cada cuatro horas	**kah**-da **k'wah**-troh **oh**-rahs
every six hours	cada seis horas	**kah**-da sace **oh**-rahs
every 4 to 6 hours	cada cuatro a seis horas	**kah**-dah **k'wah**-troh ah sace **oh**-rahs

Next, you will need to tell the patient **HOW** to take the medicine:

¿Cómo? / How?

English	Spanish	Pronunciation
as directed by your doctor	como dirigido por su doctor	ko-mo dee-ree-he-doe pour sue doke-tore
as needed…	si la necesite…	see la nay-say-see-tay
…for pain	…para el dolor	…pa-rah ale doe-lore
when you have…(pain, etc.)	cuando tenga…(dolor de, etc.)	k'wann-doe tain-gah…(doe-lore day)
only when you need it	sólo cuando lo necesite	so-lo k'wann-doe lo nay-say-see-tay
in the morning/afternoon/evening	por la mañana / tarde / noche	pour la mahn-ya-nah / tar-day / no-chay
before bedtime	antes de acostarse	ahn-tace day ah-ko-star-say
right now	ahora mismo	ah-oar-ah meece-mo
by mouth	por boca	pour bow-kah
with meals	con las comidas	cone lahs ko-me-dahs
with food	con un alimento	cone oon ah-lee-main-toe
with food	con comida	cone ko-me-dah
after meals	después de las comidas	dace-p'wace day lahs ko-me-dahs
before meals	antes de las comidas	ahn-tace day lahs ko-me-dahs
before breakfast	antes del desayuno	ahn-tace dale day-sah-you-no
after supper	después de la cena	dace-p'wace day la say-nah
with lunch	con el almuerzo	cone ale all-m'ware-so
between meals	entre las comidas	ain-tray lahs ko-me-dahs
on an empty stomach	en ayunas	ain ah-you-nahs
with water	con agua	cone ah-g'wah
mixed with food	mezclada con un alimento	mace-klah-dah cone oon ah-lee-main-toe
mixed with liquids	mezclada con líquidos	mace-klah-dah cone lee-key-dohs
when you take/eat/drink...	cuando tome...	k'wann-doe toe-may

Often, especially when getting more than one prescription, a patient does not know why he/she is taking each. This section will help you in explaining the "**Why**?"

¿Por qué? / Why?

English	Spanish	Pronunciation
for cough	para la tos	pa-rah la tohs
for infection	para la infección	pa-rah la een-fake-see-own
for nerves	para los nervios	pa-rah lohs nair-be-ohs
for stomach	para el estómago	pa-rah ale ace-toe-ma-go
for arthritis	para la artritis	pa-rah la are-tree-tiece
for circulation	para la circulación	pa-rah la seer-koo-la-see-own

for relaxing the muscles	para relajar los músculos	**pa**-rah ray-la-**har** lohs **moose**-koo-lohs
for the alleviation of pain	para aliviar el dolor	**pa**-rah ah-lee-bee-**are** ale doe-**lore**
in order to lower your…	para bajar su…	**pa**-rah ba-**harr** sue
…blood pressure	…presión de sangre	…pray-see-**own** day **sahn**-gray
…blood sugar level	…nivel de azúcar en la sangre	…nee-**bail** day ah-**sue**-car ain la **sahn**-gray

**As you can see, you can put almost anything after "para," which means "for"
You can list a body part, a symptom, a condition, a verb (aliviar = aleviate, relajar = relax, bajar = lower), etc.

OMITIR LAS DOSIS / SKIPPING DOSES

English	Spanish	Pronunciation
If you skip a dose…	Si usted omite una dosis…	see oo-**staid** oh-**mee**-tay **oo**-nah **doe**-sees…
…take it as soon as you remember.	…tómela en cuanto se acuerde.	…**toe**-may-la ain k'**wann**-toe say ah-k'**wair**-day
…wait until the next dose.	…espere hasta la siguiente dosis.	…ace-**pair**-ay ah-stah la see-**gain**-tay **doe**-sees
…Don't take an extra dose.	…No tome una dosis extra.	…no **toe**-may **oo**-nah **doe**-sees **ace**-trah

ALMACENAMIENTO / STORAGE

English	Spanish	Pronunciation
Store this medicine…	Almacene usted esta medicina….	all-ma-**say**-nay oo-**staid ace**-tah may-dee-**see**-nah
…at room temperature	..al tiempo	…all tee-**aim**-poe
…in the refrigerator	…en el refrigerador	…ain ale ray-free-hair-ah-**door**
…out of direct sunlight	…fuera de la luz del sol	…f'**wair**-ah day la loose dale soul
…out of the reach of children	…fuera del alcance de los niños	…f'**wair**-ah dale all-**kahn**-say day lohs **neen**-yohs
…away from heat	…lejos de altas temperaturas	…**lay**-hohs day **all**-tahs tame-pair-ah-**too**-rahs
…in a dry place	…en un sitio seco	…ain oon **see**-tee-oh **say**-koh
…in a cool place	…en un sitio fresco	…ain oon **see**-tee-oh **frace**-koh
Keep in original container…	Conserve en su envase original…	cone-**s'air**-bay ain sue ain-**bah**-say oh-ree-he-**nall**
…to prevent loss of…	…para evitar que pierda su…	…**pa**-rah ay-bee-**tar** kay pee-**air**-dah sue…
… potency.	…potencia.	… poe-**tain**-see-ya

OTRAS DIRECCIONES / OTHER DIRECTIONS

English	Spanish	Pronunciation
Apply	Aplique	ah-**plee**-kay
Apply externally.	Aplique externamente.	ah-**plee**-kay ace-tair-nah-**main**-tay
Apply to affected areas.	Aplique en las areas... ...afectadas.	ah-**plee**-kay ain lahs **ah**-ray-ahs... ...ah-fake-**tah**-dahs
Apply to skin.	Aplique sobre la piel.	ah-**plee**-kay **so**-bray la pee-**ale**
Apply to wound.	Aplique a la herida.	ah-**plee**-kay ah la ay-**ree**-dah
Insert	Inserte	een-**sair**-tay
Instill	Échese	**ay**-chay-say
Inject _#_ U subcutaneously.	Inyecte _#_ unidades… ...debajo de la piel.	een-**yake**-tay _#_ oo-nee-**dah**-dace… …day-**bah**-ho day la pee-**ale**
Put	Póngase	**poan**-gah-say
Place (locate)	Coloque	ko-**low**-kay
Chew	Mastique	mahs-**tee**-kay
Massage into …	Aplique con masaje	ah-**plee**-kay cone mah-**sah**-hay
Rub into…	Friccione…	freak-see-**own**-ay
Take two puffs.	Inspire dos aires.	een-**spee**-ray dohs **eye**-race
Spray…	Rocie…	**row**-see-ay
Sprinkle powder…	Rocie el polvo…	**row**-see-ay ale **pole**-bow
Swallow	Trague	**trah**-gay
Swallow it (them) whole.	Tráguela(s) entera(s).	**trah**-gay-lah(s) ain-**tay**-rah(s)
Gargle	Haga gárgaras	**ah**-gah **garr**-gah-rahs
Swish	Agite	ah-**he**-tay
Spit	Escupa	ay-**scoop**-ah
Expectorate	Expectore	ace-pake-**toe**-ray
Put it under your tongue.	Póngala debajo de la lengua.	**poan**-gah-la day-**ba**-ho day la **lane**-goo-ah
Start	Empiece	aim-pee-**ay**-say
Dilute in water.	Diluya en agua.	dee-**loo**-yah ain **ah**-g'wah
Dissolve	Disuelva	dee-**swell**-bah
Discontinue use.	Pare de tomar.	**pa**-ray day toe-**marr**
Shake well before using.	Agite bien antes de… ...cada uso.	ah-**he**-tay bee-**ain** ahn-tace day… …**kah**-dah oo-so
Close tightly after each use.	Cierre bien después de... ...cada uso.	see-**air**-ay bee-**ain** dace-**p'wace** day… …**kah**-dah oo-so
Clean	Límpiese	**leem**-pee-ay-say
Dry	Séquese	**say**-kay-say
Cover	Cubra	**koo**-brah
Tilt your head to the side.	Incline la cabeza al lado.	een-**klee**-nay lah kah-**bay**-sah ahl **lah**-doe

OTRAS DESCRIPCIONES / OTHER DESCRIPTIONS

English	Spanish	Pronunciation
left	izquierdo/a	ee-ski-**air**-doe / ah
right	derecho/a	day-**ray**-choe / ah
both	ambos/as / los/las dos	**ahm**-bohs / ahs / lohs/lahs dohs
each	cada	**kah**-dah
liberally	Libremente	**lee**-bray-**main**-tay
sparingly	una pequeña cantidad	**oo**-nah pay-**cane**-yah kahn-tee-**dod**
lightly	Ligeramente	lee-**hair**-ah-**main**-tay

OTRAS ADVERTENCIAS / OTHER WARNINGS

English	Spanish	Pronunciation
Avoid alcohol while taking this medicine.	Evite usted el alcohol mientras que toma esta medicina.	ay-**bee**-tay oo-**staid** ale all-koh-**ole** me-**ain**-trahs kay toe-**ma ace**-tah may-dee-**see**-nah
Don't drive while …taking this medicine.	No conduzca mientras que …toma esta medicina.	no cone-**doose**-kah me-**ain**-trahs kay …toe-**ma ace**-tah may-dee-**see**-nah
Don't take aspirin without … your doctor knowing it.	No tome aspirina sin …saberlo su doctor.	no **toe**-may ahs-pee-**ree**-nah seen …sah-**bare**-lo su doke-**tore**
Avoid milk, antacids and …iron one hour before …taking this medicine.	No tome leche, antiácido o …hierro dentro de una hora de …tomar esta medicina.	no **toe**-may **lay**-chay, ahn-tee-**ah**-see-doe oh …**yair**-oh **dane**-troh day **oo**-nah **oh**-rah day …toe-**mar ace**-tah may-dee-**see**-nah
Avoid the sun while taking this medicine.	Evite usted el sol mientras que está tomando esta medicina.	ay-**bee**-tay oo-**staid** ale soul me-**ain**-trahs kay ace-**tah** toe-**mahn**-doe **ace**-tah may-dee-**see**-nah
Do not take this medicine if …you are pregnant.	No tome esta medicina si …está embarazada.	no **toe**-may **ace**-tah may-dee-**see**-nah see …ace-**tah** aim-bar-ah-**sah**-dah
External use only.	Para uso externo solamente.	**pa**-rah **oo**-so ace-**tair**-no so-la-**main**-tay
Call us with questions or …problems.	Llámenos con preguntas o …problemas.	**ya**-may-nohs cone pray-**goon**-gahs oh …pro-**blay**-mahs
Call your doctor if you have problems.	Llame a su doctor si tenga problemas.	**yah**-may ah sue doke-**tore** see **tain**-gah pro-**blay**-mahs
Stop taking the medicine if…	Deje de tomar el medicamento si…	**day**-hay day toe-**mar** ale may-dee-kah-**main**-toe see…
Don't use after this date:___	No use después de esta fecha:___	no **oo**-say dace-**p'wace** day **ace**-tah **fay**-chah:___

Don't take this medicine	No tome este medicamento	no **toe**-may **ace**-tay may-dee-kah-**main**-toe
…at the same time as other	… al mismo tiempo con otros	…all **mees**-mo tee-**aim**-poe cone **oh**-trohs
…medicines.	…medicamentos.	…may-dee-kah-**main**-tohs

EJEMPLOS DE DIRECCIONES PARA LAS RECETAS
SAMPLE DIRECTIONS FOR USE:

These combinations of directions were requested by course participants.

English	Spanish	Pronunciation
Take one tablet	Tome una tableta	**toe**-may **oo**-nah tah-**blay**-tah
…three times a day	…tres veces al día	…trace **base**-ace all **dee**-ah
…for seven days	…por siete días	…pour see-**ay**-tay **dee**-ahs
…until gone.	…hasta que no hay más.	…**ah**-stah kay no eye mahs
…Then, take…	…Luego, tome…	…loo-**ay**-go **toe**-may…
Take two tablets	Tome dos tabletas	**toe**-may dohs tah-**blay**-tahs
…two times a day	…dos veces al día	…dohs **base**-ace all **dee**-ah
…with food	…con alimento	…cone ah-lee-**main**-toe
…for seven days	…por siete días	…pour see-**ay**-tay **dee**-ahs
…in each month.	…de cada mes.	…day **kah**-dah mace
…Skip three months.	…No las tome por tres meses.	…no lahs **toe**-may pour trace **mace**-ace
…Repeat.	…Repita.	…ray-**pee**-tah

¡Practiquemos! / Let's Practice!

Actividad III: Put these directions for use into the correct order (take, quantity, frequency, reason).

| una cucharada | para la tos | cada ocho horas | tome |

(Use components above and write directions below).

Directions:_____.

| dos veces al día | tome | una tableta | para la infección |

Directions:_____.

| tome | con comida | si las necesite para el dolor | dos tabletas |

Directions:_____.

| una vez al día | una píldora | tome | hasta que no hay más |

Directions:_____.

ANSWERS:

| una cucharada | para la tos | cada ocho horas | tome |

Directions: **Tome una cucharada cada ocho horas para la tos.**

| dos veces al día | tome | una tableta | para la infección |

Directions: **Tome una tableta dos veces al día para la infección.**

| tome | con comida | si las necesite para el dolor | dos tabletas |

Directions: **Tome dos tabletas con comida si las necesite para el dolor.**

| una vez al día | una píldora | tome | hasta que no hay más |

Directions: **Tome una píldora una vez al día hasta que no hay más.**

Actividad IV: Translate the following directions for use into Spanish. You may write each on a piece of paper or type it on your electronic device and check your answers afterwards.

- Take one tablet three times a day until gone. If you skip a dose take it as soon as you remember.
- Clean and dry the affected area. Apply sparingly three times a day or as directed by your doctor. Cover the affected area with a bandage. External use only.
- Take two teaspoons every six hours as needed for cough. Avoid alcohol while taking this medicine. Don't drive while taking this medicine.
- Tilt head to the side. Apply 2 drops to left ear as needed for pain. Close tightly after each use.

COMPLETE PRACTICE ACTIVITY BEFORE PROCEEDING TO NEXT PAGE.
ANSWERS FOLLOW.

Answers:

- Tome una tableta tres veces al día hasta que no hay más. Si usted omite una dosis, tómela en cuanto se acuerde.
- Límpiese y séquese la area afectada. Aplique una pequeña cantidad tres veces al día o como dirigido por su doctor. Cubra la area afectada con un vendaje. Para uso externo solo / solamente.
- Tome dos cucharitas / cucharaditas cada seis horas si / como la necesite para la tos. Evite usted el alcohol mientras que toma (está tomando) esta medicina. No conduzca mientras que toma (está tomando) esta medicina.
- Incline la cabeza al lado. Aplique dos gotas a la oreja izquierda si / como la necesite para el dolor. Cierre bien después de cada uso.

Actividad V: Sample Dialogues

In this exercise, you will be prompted for the Pharmacist's responses to the patient questions and statements. (**You will need to listen to the digital audio** mp3s, the audio CDs or the audio in the online program **for this exercise.**)

This is an oral exercise that pulls together the information from this lesson and gives you real-life scenarios for practice. You will not have a written guide for this portion. It is meant to mimic a real-life scenario in which you are speaking with a Spanish-speaking patient. Try to do this exercise without writing down anything. If you need to hear something again, simply rewind this audio and play it again. After all, in real life, you can say, "Repita, por favor" or "Otra vez."

Written Information/Patient Information

In addition to using these words and phrases orally, you can write them on forms and/or signs. Here are a few helpful phrases:

Consultation area	Las consultas
Pick-up prescriptions here.	Puede recoger las recetas aquí.
Drop-off prescriptions here.	Puede dejar las recetas aquí.

**Hands on Spanish grants permission to reproduce the next two pages to use as patient information sheets in your pharmacy. Where the English translations do not appear on the following patient information sheet, you will find them in the actual text of this course.

Whenever possible, we fill prescriptions with generic medications. They are less expensive and are approved by the FDA. Please let us know if you prefer namebrand medications.

Cuando sea posible, surtimos las recetas con medicinas genéricas. Son más baratas y aprobadas por la Administración de Medicinas y Comestibles. Por favor, díganos si usted prefiere las medicinas de marca registrada.

Confidential Patient Information Sheet
Hoja Confidencial de Información sobre el/la Paciente

Please complete this form so that we can check your prescriptions against health conditions and drug allergies. This information will remain confidential. It is your responsibility to update this information. Thank you. **Por favor, llene esta forma para que podamos revisar sus recetas contra ciertas condiciones y alergias que usted tiene. Esta información es confidencial. La responsabilidad de poner al día esta información es suya. Gracias.**

Full name/**el nombre completo** _____
                last/**apellido(s)**   first/**nombre(s)**

Address/**dirección** _____

City/**ciudad** _____ State/**estado** _____ Zip code/**zona postal** _____

Home phone/**número del teléfono de su casa** ( ) _____

Work phone/**número del teléfono de su trabajo** ( ) _____

Date of birth/**fecha de nacimiento** _____/_____/_____
                                      mes   fecha   año

Sex/**sexo** _____

D.L.# or S.S. #/**número de su licencia de conducir o de seguro social** _____

DRUG ALLERGIES / ALERGIAS A MEDICINAS

ninguna _____
(none)

aspirina_____
(aspirin)

cefalosporina_____
(cephalosporin)

codeína_____
(codeine)

eritromicina_____
(erythromycin)

penicilina_____
(penicillin)

medicamento basado en azufre_____
(sulfur based medication)

tetracyclina_____
(tetracycline)

otra _____
(other)

MEDICAL CONDITIONS / CONDICIONES MÉDICAS

____asma
____glaucoma
____migraña
____epilepsia
____está embarazada
____le da de pecho

____angina
____úlceras
____cáncer
____diabetes

____hipertensión/alta presión arterial
____condición del tiroideo
____condición del corazón
____condición respiratoria
____condición de la próstata
____otra(s)_____
_____
_____

MEDICATIONS THAT YOU ARE TAKING/MEDICAMENTOS QUE ESTÁ TOMANDO
(...PRESCRIPTION & NON-PRESCRIPTION/...QUE NECESITA RECETA Y NO)

_____

_____

_____

OTHER QUESTIONS/OTRAS PREGUNTAS

1. ¿Tiene usted una tarjeta de seguro médico?   sí_____ no_____
   (Por favor, dénos la tarjeta con esta forma.)
Do you have an insurance card? If so, leave it with us.

2. ¿Prefiere usted que surtamos la receta con la forma genérica?   sí_____ no_____
Do you prefer generic drugs?

3. ¿Prefiere usted que pongamos una tapa a prueba de los niños? sí_____ no_____
Do you prefer a child-proof cap?

4. ¿Fuma usted?   sí_____ no_____
Do you smoke?

5. ¿Toma usted el alcohol?   sí_____ no_____
   Do you drink alcohol?

La firma_____   La fecha ____/____/____

CONCLUSION:

You have learned an incredible amount in a short period of time. Do not try to memorize all of this at once. Studies show that memory retention is much better when you study in smaller increments more frequently.

Remember that perfect practice makes perfect, so continue to practice improving pronunciation and structuring your sentences. Practice as often as possible on the job. You will then learn in the most natural of ways: you will first learn those things that you say the most often. You will be guided by necessity, which is the most powerful motivator! Also, do not be afraid to make mistakes; we learn from them. Do not wait until your Spanish is perfect before you practice it. It will never get there without practice. Enjoy your new language!

I would like to say a **special thanks** to my husband, Chris, for his constant support and encouragement. His skills as a computer programmer were the driving force behind our release of Pharmacy Spanish as an online course. His talents are priceless to my company and his love is priceless to me.

I would like to thank my children, Emery and Maya, both adopted from Colombia, for inspiring me to reach out further to our Hispanic community in the U.S.

I thank my parents, Harry and Tricia Hinton, for their continual support and for the wonderful example they have set. I thank my sisters, Natalie Phillips and Jessica Hinton, both of whom are registered nurses, for answering my every medical question pertaining to the development of my courses.

I would also like to thank Trina von Waldner, Pharm. D., the Director of Postgraduate Continuing Education of the University of Georgia's College of Pharmacy, for her constant guidance and assistance with the ACPE accreditation of the online program.

Most of all, I would like to thank the God who bestowed the talents upon me to make this possible.

"I can do all things through Christ who strengthens me." Philippians 4:13

¡Buena suerte!